LIFECLOCK

Bruno and Louise Huber are the founders of ASTROLOGISCH-PSYCHOLOGISCHES INSTITUT in Adliswil/Zurich, Switzerland. In addition to a personal counseling practice, they teach astrology at the institute, in England, as well as lecturing throughout the world. Both have been keynote speakers at the American Federation of Astrologers Convention for the past several conferences, and they host the now-famous international World Congress in astrology at Lucerne.

LIFECLOCK

Practical Techniques for Counseling Age Progression in the Horoscope

volume 2

> Including the Age Progression
> applied to the horoscope of C.G. Jung
> written by Werner Stephan

BRUNO & LOUISE HUBER

SAMUEL WEISER, INC.
York Beach, Maine

First published in German in 1983 by Verlag Astrologisch-Psychologisches Institut Adliswil/Zurich under the title: *Lebensuhr im Horoskop: Alterprogressions-Methode*
© 1983 Bruno and Louise Huber

First published in English by
Samuel Weiser, Inc.
Box 612
York Beach, ME 03910

ISBN 0-87728-609-4
Library of Congress Catalog Card Number: 82-50533

Typeset in 10 point Baskerville
Printed in the United States of America

Contents

Acknowledgments

To all the friends who devote themselves so unreservedly to our Work and are always there when needed, we should like to express our warmest thanks. Our gratitude is also due to our colleagues for their active help in the preparation of this book.

Mirjam Bertsch
Daniel Cuny
Marianne Egli
Dr. Maja Hodler
Michael-A. Huber
Margrit Huser-Schwaninger
Rita Keller
Johanna Kohler
John Portmann
Jak Riger
Lilian Schatz
Max Senn
Werner Stephan
Irene Wieser
Lydia Wittlin

And we should also like to thank for their patience all those who have waited so long for this book to appear.

Symbols of the planets

Sun	☉	♂		Mars
Moon	☽	♃		Jupiter
Saturn	♄	♅ (♅)		Uranus
Mercury	☿	♆		Neptune
Venus	♀	♈ (♇)		Pluto
Dragon's Head	☊			

Symbols of the Signs

Aries	♈	♎		Libra
Taurus	♉	♏		Scorpio
Gemini	♊	♐		Sagittarius
Cancer	♋	♑		Capricorn
Leo	♌	♒		Aquarius
Virgo	♍	♓		Pisces

Abbreviations

AC = Ascendant   AP = Age Point
IC = Imum Coeli   HC = House Cusp
DC = Descendant   LP = Low Point
MC = Medium Coeli   IP = Invert Point

Synonyms: Age Progression, Hand on the Life Clock, Age Point (AP)

Dedication

"Die Zeit vergeht, und die Weisheit bleibt.
Sie wechselt ihre Formen und Riten, aber sie beruht
zu allen Zeiten auf demselben Fundament: auf
die Einordnung des Menschen in die Natur, in
den kosmischen Rhythmus."

Hermann Hesse

Time moves on, but Wisdom remains. She varies
her forms and rites, yet rests in every period
on one and the same foundation: the incorporation
of Mankind in Nature, in the rhythm of the Cosmos.

Note to the Reader

In the last few years much new knowledge has been won in regard to the application of the Age Progression method, and we can now take a look at it in this second volume. In Volume 1 we presented full details of the structure, mode of action, and technique of Age Progression, as well as the phases and cycles in life and in the horoscope. In Volume 2 we can concentrate on how all these rules work in practice. In order to bring the dry bones of the subject to life, we include interesting case histories, and present a new way of looking at aspects which you will find useful when reading your own horoscope. Considerable attention is devoted to the meanings of the planets, and this has been done quite deliberately so that you can work out what is likely to happen when the Age Point transits a planetary position. This will enable you to obtain the greatest possible help from Age Progressions, both in daily life and in your astrological studies. Above all you will be persuaded of the correctness of the method. It has been very satisfying to hear—from many in the astrological fraternity and from lay people alike—how well the Age Point corresponds to life. And you have only to read the biography of C.G. Jung as given in this book to reach the same conclusion.

There is still much to add on the subject of Age Progression as a new science of biological cycles. The present volume is by no means a full statement of everything known about it and a third volume entitled *The Spiritual Meaning of the Age Point* has just been published in German.

Bruno and Louise Huber

Part I

**How to Apply
the Age Point Method**

Chapter 1

Overview of Volume One

Introduction—Comparable methods—The technique—Retrospect—Spatial rhythms, temporal rhythms, life rhythms—Temporal dimension in the horoscope—Life cycles—Time sectors—Experiences matter more than events—Points the AP helps to clarify.

● Introduction

The first volume in this series has been widely acclaimed. Time and again it was confirmed that with the aid of the new Age Progression Method, exceptionally accurate and interesting statements could be made. Time and again this method has "hit the nail on the head" in greater or lesser ways and, what is more, it has shown itself capable of revealing underlying strands of meaning running through life. It is very easy to use. After a little practice, anyone can tell from one glance at his horoscope just where he is in life and the reason for his current situation. A quick survey can be made of the whole life, without resort to complicated calculations.

Bruno Huber, the well-known astrologer and psychologist based in Switzerland, has developed and proved the Age Progression method in his long-established teaching and consulting work. It has been employed with success since 1973 by many students of astrological psychology (including physicians, psychologists, social workers and educators). Mankind has always been fascinated by the topic of life cycles and the "Ages of Man," but until now no one has succeeded in presenting a simple yet exact method applicable to the individual horoscope and open to use by anybody.

Comparable methods

In a bygone century a method already existed employing, not the six-year rhythm of Age Progression, but one of five years per house. A French clergyman, *Pater Yves*, described in 1654 in his book *Nova Methodus*, a sixty-year cycle through the Placidus Houses. In our own century, the German astrologer *A. Frank Glahn* of Hamburg experimented (rather fruitlessly it would seem) with a life cycle of one hundred years read clockwise on the chart, that is to say against the normal run of the houses. Since 1956 the Munich astrologer *Wolfgang Döbereiner* has been teaching a similar system, though instead of one hundred years, he has adopted a life-span of eighty-four years—again taken clockwise round the chart. In 1932, *C.C. Schneider* published in an astrological magazine an article on the life cycle, proposing that this moved in seventy-two years by six-year stages through the areas of the horoscope. However, he made no specific assertions. *Wilhelmine* and *Arnold Keyserling* of Vienna have developed a method that comes closest to Age Progression. They move in a seven-year rhythm from house to house and stress that, with changes of sign and transits of planetary positions, there occur noticeable changes in the native's comportment.

The Age Progression method as proposed here describes our life through the twelve houses in a six-year rhythm (calculated according to the Koch House System). During the course of our life we travel through our own horoscope and experience the characteristic effects of the planets, signs and houses at times which may be precisely determined. Using an appropriate method, we can therefore make differentiated statements in such matters as how the personality will unfold, the significance of changes and crises in consciousness for spiritual growth, which hindrances to the individuation process have to be overcome, and much more. Our intention is to concentrate on the basic psychological situation and on the individual plan of development in man, not on future events. This is one essential difference between the more usual methods of progression and our method.

Traditional methods

In the traditional methods of prognosis, practically exclusive use is made of *planetary transits* in order to determine coming influences. The positions of the planets at some given point in time are determined and so are the aspects they throw from these new positions to the planets in the natal chart. Inferences are then made concerning the good or bad luck to be expected in the near future. Generally speaking, however, it is impossible to integrate these frequently conflicting aspects. And it is even harder, if Age Progression is not used, to ascertain which of the transits are important for the individual concerned and which are not. When other methods of progression are employed as well—*axial directions* or *progressed planets*—the upshot of hours of careful study of the horoscope can be much confusion but little benefit. Mixing methods makes it difficult to evaluate the situation as a whole.

In contrast to the above, the Age Progression Method relies on a single element: the Age Point. This method makes use of a time mechanism present in the horoscope itself. As the hand swings round on the "clock of life," the planetary positions, signs, and houses light up one after another, and show the leading influences at every stage.

The technique

The technique is a simple one and can be grasped immediately. Life starts at the Ascendant. The hand on the life-clock begins moving counterclockwise, that is to say it follows the sequence of the houses from one to twelve. Commencing with the AC as zero, we

Figure 1.1.1. The path of the Age Point through the houses.

proceed through all twelve houses as shown in figure 1.1.1. At the cusp of the second house we are six years old, at the third cusp we are twelve, at the fourth cusp or IC we are eighteen, and so on, regardless of how big or small a particular house may be. At the age of seventy-two we have returned to the Ascendant; at seventy-eight we are back at cusp two, etc. To obtain the annual movement merely count the number of degrees in the relevant house and divide by six.[1]

Koch Houses

There are various house systems in astrology. Therefore before you start using Age Progression you should make sure which house system is employed in your chart. Those most often favored today are those of Dr. Koch, Placidus, Campanus and the Equal House system. We have chosen Dr. Walter Koch's Birth-place Houses because these are the only ones which give correct results with Age Progression. The house division, already described in Vol. 1, is much the same as in other systems, the main difference being the placements of the intermediate cusps. These placements are, however, crucial.

Retrospect

The discovery of the Age Point some twenty years ago, at the Institute for Psychosynthesis run by Professor Roberto Assagioli in Florence, happened almost by chance. During a very intensive piece of research (in which house systems were compared, the Low Point identified, etc.) Bruno Huber examined many individual natal charts. One day he noticed a remarkable number of changes of occupation in certain of the natives. Although the reasons for such intended or effected changes differed widely, they did have one thing in common: roughly in the middle of the sixth house in each map lay the dividing line between two signs. Without reference for the moment to the tenth house (of public position) it became obvious that in the sixth house (of work and the struggle for existence) there was a regular change of sign as, for example, from Libra in the first half to Scorpio in the second. (See figure 1.1.2.) What is more, all those concerned were in their thirties and had reached the half-way stage in their lives. So here was a double halving (a halving of the

---

[1]For further information, see pages 37-41 of *Life Clock*, Volume 1, Samuel Weiser, York Beach, ME, 1982.

Figure 1.1.2. The Age Point is significant when the signs change mid-house, indicating important stages of life.

house corresponding to the halving of the life); plainly some time mechanism was in operation. This was where work on the problem really started. What was required was to find the mathematical quantity (the time unit) that might be underlying the mechanism. An extensive series of calculations led to the conclusion that, when the sixth house was divided into seventy-two parts corresponding to a presumed life-span of seventy-two years, any border separating two signs in the sixth house always coincided with the age at which the native changed his occupation or at least seriously considered doing so.

Bruno Huber was able to confirm this important discovery by testing it in situations not directly related to the occupation: for example, familial changes intimated in the fourth house, change of dwelling and emigration in houses three and nine, changes in relative prosperity in houses two and eight. He found invariably that where there was some alteration in the course of a life, a shift in sign occurred in the corresponding house, not at any old time but at the very time, measured on the seventy-two year scale, when the said alteration occurred. He dubbed this *exact* place in the house the *Age Point.*

In keeping with the law of analogy enshrined in the well-known esoteric dictum "as above so below" a further discovery was made. The time-scale of seventy-two years could be employed not only in the *micro* single house but also in the *macro* whole horoscope as a standard of measurement. Hence there is a bigger Age Point moving over the entire circle of the horoscope in seventy-two years, which divided by twelve gives a stay of six years in each house (further information on the cosmic number 72 can be found in Vol. 1, p. 30 ff).

The results of countless case studies where this mechanism was recognized were breath-taking, and it was found that in addition to the cross-overs between the signs, the transits of the Age Point over the house cusps, Low Points and planets were also relevant. Other aspects (oppositions, trines, etc.) between the Age Point and the planets were significant too. Therefore the Age Point is comparable to the hand of a clock. It sets out from the cusp of the first house (on the Ascendant) and during a period of seventy-two years makes constantly new aspects with all the prominent points in the horoscope.

House rhythm, time rhythm, life rhythm

In interpreting the horoscope we are accustomed to thinking in terms of the houses. A Moon posited on the left-hand side of the chart in the fourth quadrant is regarded as introverted and definitely different from a Moon on the right-hand, extrovert side. Or, we take it for granted that a person with aspects mainly formed in the lower half of the horoscope is less aware of his motivations than is someone whose planets are concentrated in the upper half. Furthermore, the houses represent spatial regions for us: twelve different spheres of existence with their own themes and no ranking among themselves. When, to stay with our given example, we are studying "change of occupation" we interrogate the sixth house and, if necessary, the tenth (with its theme of the career). We are hardly likely to look for information on occupational possibilities in the twelfth house of retirement and cosmic attachment. Obviously this type of approach is space-oriented, it is concerned with rhythm in space. Until now, the time dimension has been introduced in the horoscope solely through transits and progressions. These work in a more or less complicated manner with elements lying outside the horoscope which project their influence into it. How different, however, is the six-year rhythm of the Age Point—a time mechanism inherent in the horoscope which, like the planets, aspects, signs and houses, forms a natural part of it and is an essential component in interpretation!

The time dimension in the horoscope

In everyday life we frequently encounter time as a negative factor. We find that we do things at the wrong time, that on the whole we have too little time, that we grow old too soon. Time then is a fact of life of which we become conscious only when it obtrudes itself on us unpleasantly.

We are much less aware that time is constantly in motion, ceaselessly flowing out of the past into the future, and that the present in the midst of these is not an isolated unit. Admittedly we experience the present at every moment, but we are also able to enhance each moment with memories of the past and with anticipations of the future, and to perceive it in its spatial, geographical dimension; to get to know it in fact as a "total association." It is all the more important therefore to break out of our space-orientated here-and-now way of looking at things and to get the feel of the flow of time.

Time does not start, it does not stop, and because of its sheer continuity is hard to grasp. All we can do is to seize on a few present moments as they pass along its endless conveyor belt and to store them in our memories. But time is more than this. There is a vital dimension in it, symbolized in the horoscope by the circular path turning back into itself; there is a *Significance* deeper than the stringing together of isolated time points. Time tends to develop!

If only we could succeed in taking hold of all the developmental possibilities brought to us by time in its perpetual flow and could incorporate them in the spatial dimension of our experience, we should loose ourselves from the "tyranny of the moment." We should shake free from inflexible determinism to take advantage of ever newly available possibilities. Having become actively aware of all the dimensions enfolded in the present, we should have the power to change our futures.

This spatial view of time gives us the opportunity to use Age Progression creatively and to see human freedom and fate in more holistic terms. External and internal events can be integrated with the (multi-relational) totality of life, and assimilation be deeper and more aware. What is more, the planetary constellations highlighted one after another by the moving Age Point can be seen in their bearing on past and present as well as on the future. In other words, they become sign-posts along the road to self-determination.

Thus the horoscope, when studied in its tempero-spatial connections, enables us to grasp fate and character in the aggregate. By getting to know the causality of our Karma we can better perform our Dharma, and so evolve in a productive way.[2]

Admittedly, the complexity of our own make-up binds us to a great extent, and this is reflected in the determinism in our personal horoscopes. A plant which grows from a daisy seed will never turn into a poppy. Nevertheless, a frank acceptance of the way in which life has to develop does not exclude gradual change. Change comes, and it is mutation, it is growth, it is the attainment of new life-forms and qualities.

A preset consciousness and the hand of fate fashion each moment of life and decide whether and how change will occur in the course of time. Hours, days and years are taken in prospect, and the future is moulded in the now. When consciously assimilated, the past may enter into this process in the form of experience, and show us how the linear chain of life's moments joins up into whole sections of life and becomes part of the full circle of the horoscope.

Life cycles

The development of men and women tends to follow a basic pattern. In infancy and youth we are all linked by common principles of development and go through the same phases. Yet, equally, each of our lives has its own unique character and pursues its own special way.

Life is like a journey whose starting point is birth and whose end point is death. No one can avoid making the trip, but there are many cultural, social and individual detours on the way. The time-scale can be extended or compressed within certain limits, and in extreme cases the journey can come to a complete halt.

The process of develoment is no easy, unbroken, even flow. There are various times, good and bad, with happy and not so happy hours. Each of us has some notion of periods within the life cycle. These periods can be found in the horoscope itself. The Age Progression method divides the house system into twelve large time

---

[2]Karma and Dharma are two Sanskrit words which have acquired a technical sense in Indian philosophy. Here it would be safe to render Karma as circumstances, and Dharma as duty, though more strictly speaking the first means action and the second means law. *Tr.*

sectors and the individual houses into three smaller time sectors (see Vol. 1, pp. 66-67). This provides us with thirty-six different time qualities; for each of these sections has a quite specific character and is distinct from the one which precedes it and from the one which follows. The concept of time takes many forms. We have only to think of the seasons: spring is a time of awakening when everything is in bloom; winter is a time of death, and also of rebirth, standing as it does at the beginning of a new cycle. Then there are the times of day: daybreak, noon, twilight and the dark still night—and each has its special, recurring, atmospheric and psychological features. Even the ancients have left us representations of the connection between the seasons and the phases of the human life cycle. The Greeks early on divided the horoscope into the four seasons.

Time sectors

When we talk of time sectors we are implying that the course of life has a definite structure and that it follows certain guidelines. Life's development can be regarded as a series of identifiable time factors, corresponding to the themes of the twelve astrological houses. A time sector is a relatively stable part of the whole life cycle, just as a house is of the entire house system, but a significant change does occur in each sector and house.

No time sector is better or more important than another: each contributes something to the character of the life cycle of which it is an organic part. Each contains in miniature the past and the future in combination. And the series of sectors is a macro-structure of the entire life cycle, a framework for the processes of development in everyday life.

Experiences matter more than events

From what has already been said, it will be clear not only that the Age Point is a very important time factor in the horoscope, but also that its significance in the various houses can sharpen our understanding. It enables us to enter into the inner meaning of an individual's progress through life. And in doing so we quickly discover that what is of paramount importance are not the isolated events but the experiences to which they give rise.

The distinction is a crucial one. Some methods of progression confine attention to certain outstanding incidents. The concern of the Age Point Method is with a person's experience, those psychic events which have a transforming effect. An extremely dramatic episode can be played out and leave little impression behind it and, on the other hand, a profound, spiritual experience may take place over many months, without a corresponding chord being struck in the external world. But in any case, between these extremes, there are events in every human life which are accompanied by intense inner experiences.

In general, only by consciously recognizing the process can we see what sense they make in life's wider context. And then it is not merely the psychic happenings that count, but what we have learned from them. In other words, the consequences of external events have to be faced; we have to come to grips with each suddenly activated psychic constellation, or, to put it yet another way, we look for the whys and wherefores and then recognize the inner forces applied by the individual constitution to a specific situation.

Right here the Age Point can help us to graduate from general character reading to true insight into experience and behavior; and this it does as its position in sign and house activates aspects to given planets.

● Points the Age Point
Helps Us to Clarify

It is instructive to study the effect on our lives as the gound-themes of the individual houses come into focus. We can make a better assessment of the influences of transits and progressions.

1. We come to realize how one-sided our view of the universe has been—the extent to which we tend to choose to do (or to accept) only those things immediately interesting to us, and to ignore other things.

2. With one glance at our charts we can identify the area, sign or house that currently concerns us, our present problems, and our chances of solving them.

   a) As soon as the AP approaches a planetary position, we notice an intensification of development on which we can focus beforehand (according to the nature of the planet in question).

b) When the Age Point transits a house cusp or one of the two sensitive points (the Invert Point and the Low Point), it signals heightened readiness for action if the house cusp is involved, long-term planning if the Invert Point is involved, and a pause to take fresh bearings if the Low Point is involved.

c) When the Age Point crosses from one zodiac sign into another, there is a change in our temperament, in our attitude, and in the type and method of our performance, corresponding to the nature of the new sign. Since it is possible to calculate the sign our Age Point will occupy at any given period in our lives, we can allow for it in advance.

3. The Age Point can be used to give us an overview of past, present and future. It can show us which actions and attitudes in the past have brought about our present situation, and can give us a lead on what to do in order to overcome difficulties and to encourage the growth of what is only weakly developed.

4. We can uncover traumatic events in our childhood which have left their imprint on our lives, and can identify those faults in our characters which have been caused by them. This enables us to take steps to try and correct the faults.

These are a few of the possibilities and advantages offered to us by employment of the Age Point. We shall now take a look into this material in greater depth and, by giving different case notes in the second part of this book, shall endeavor to show how it may be used in practice.

Chapter 2

Rules of Interpretation

High and Low Points in Age Progression—The duration of the High and Low Points—Three phases in each house—The three Quadruplicities operative in each house—Life's episodes—Structural changes—Advance influence of the cusps—Angular, Succedent and Cadent cusps—Advance influence of the planets upon sign entry—Signs without Low Points—Signs with two house cusps—Intercepted signs—Passage of AP through empty houses—Aspect holes—Distance Halving: turning points—Change of configurations—The significance of secondary aspecting in configurational change—Passage of AP through heavily tenanted houses—Stellium—Cycles involving transits and progressions—Joint action of transits and AP—Transit-AP relationships—Cycles in tandem with transiting and progressed planets—The AP and slow transits.

We have already presented Rules for Application of the Age Point, important rules of analysis in some detail. We now wish to enter into these rules more fully. (See *Life Clock*, Vol. 1, pp. 53-64.)

● Rule 1: High and Low Points in Age Progression

Each house is divided into three regions by the intensity curve; there are entered via the house cusp, the Invert Point and the Low Point. This creates a cyclic rhythm of the Age Point with natural crests and troughs (see also Vol. 1, p. 49). We experience the high

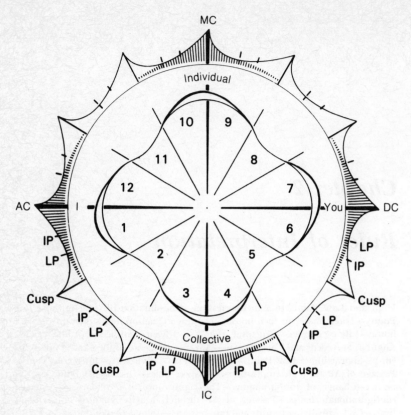

Figure 1.2.1. The intensity curve.

points at the house cusps (HC), the low points at the appropriately named Low Points (LP = golden mean) of houses.[1] See figure 1.2.1. It is of course important to know the time durations of the high and low points.

The high points last from the house cusps to the Invert Point (IP). The Age Point traverses this stretch within 2 years, 3 months and 15 days. From the house cusp to the Low Point the time taken is 3 years, 8 months and 15 days, or almost 4 years. Experience teaches that the Low Point starts to take effect as much as 8 months before

---

[1]See Bruno and Louise Huber, *The Astrological Houses*, Samuel Weiser, York Beach, ME, 1984. First published under the title of *Man and His World*, 1978.

exact transit by the Age Point, and so we speak of a "Low-Point Year." The space of time from the Low Point to the next cusp is therefore barely 2 years, 3 months and 15 days.

Taken together, these phases give six years for each house. The two extreme regions (the cusp and the Low Point) plainly differ from one another in qualities: the first is a phase of construction and action, the second is a phase of retrenchment and rest. The transit of the Age Point over the LP positions brings times of introspection, of turning inwards, whereas transits over cusps motivate us to summon all our powers to achieve external goals—though in different ways according to the natures of the crosses: cardinal, fixed and mutable.

● Rule 2: Phases in Each House

Accordingly in each house we find three different phases (see figure 1.2.2), in which the high and low points stand out most clearly. This tripartite division provides us with information on smaller life cycles. As is well-known, the three quadruplicities are essential to an understanding in astrology of basic human motivation. The principle of cardinality motivates us to exert our will power to become an achiever, the principle of fixity craves for security in order to conserve what has been produced, and the principle of mutability is always looking for something new with a view to abandoning static conditions and recommending develop-

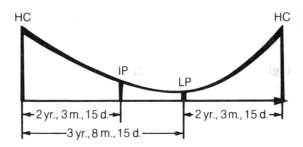

Figure 1.2.2. The house broken into Invert Point and Low Point periods.

ment (see also Vol. 1, pp. 100 and 143-44). In accordance with the analogy "That which is above is as that which is below" we shall apply the same division to the individual houses.

The Quadruplicities in each house

If we superimpose the quadruplicities on the three regions in each house, a picture emerges such as we see in figure 1.2.3. The region following the cusp corresponds to the cardinal quality. Here we find it relatively easy to devote our energies to external matters. At the Invert Point we reach the Fixed region of the house and encounter a braking effect, and at the Low Point (LP) our energies tend to touch zero as far as our outer life is concerned; they are still present but are turned inwards.

After this the curve turns upwards, and we find ourselves in the mutable region of the house, which usually requires some form of adjustment or reorientation on our part. The cuspal influence which accords so well with the cardinal quality, is experienced most intensely in the cardinal houses (one, four, seven and ten). The Low Point experience corresponds to that of the Fixed Cross, and so stagnation and the introversion of energy are most clearly traceable in the four fixed houses (two, five, eight and eleven). Finally, the theme of mutability is expressed most strongly at the Low Points of the mutable houses (three, six, nine and twelve).

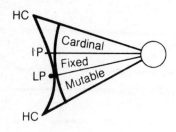

Figure 1.2.3. Each house has a cardinal, fixed, and mutable quality contained within it.

Life's episodes

During the course of our lives we experience these episodes in an invariable rhythm. An impulse to engage in fresh undertakings is always present at the house cusps; active achievement is the order of the day. When we concentrate on our aims, greater success can be achieved than at other times. For two years we are fairly successful. At the Invert Point our energies are brought to the right pitch and goals towards which we have been working can now be reached. As we aproach the Low Point, our activities begin to die away. At the end of the phase of movement, not quite four years after the axial impulse, our energies come to a state of repose at the Low Point. In comparison with the previous period, we often have a feeling of failure. It is a time for taking stock. Furthermore, the Low Points signal a reorientation or a development crisis, all according to the way we react to them. More will be said about this in the chapter on "Low Point Experiences in the Crosses as Doors to the Inner Self," in Vol. 3. Here we would merely observe that whoever deals properly with the Low Points and learns the message coming from within, will find life easier at the next house cusp. Neglect to turn inwards and a lack of insight into how life is motivated will give a harder climb to the following cusp.

Structural changes

Looking at it another way, this three-phase develement process brings about a progressive change in our behavior structure. At the commencement of a stage of development or a new cycle, which generally means at the cusp of a house, we have plenty of energy and potential available to us, but a proportionately limited structure. Our behavioral repertoire is small as yet, and our adaptability is narrow in scope—we expend a large amoung of energy on our personal concerns. Nevertheless, as time goes on and we approach the Invert Point, our behavior becomes more structured and includes an increasing number of components, making possible an increasingly differentiated approach to the business of life. In the fixed phase of the house, all the components and capacities are integrated into a complex arrangement. The structure becomes more stable, and functions for a period in the fixed region, but then slowly disintegrates until it finally falls apart at the Low Point to give way to some new form.

● Rule 3: Advance Influence of the Cusps

A further rule of interpretation of the AP is the following:

It is not only the exact moment when an axis is transited that is important, but also the build-up time, especially the phase before the cusp.

This pre-cuspal phase is usually a stressful time, especially in the short section before the poles of the main AC/DC and IC/MC axes. Here we enter the wake of the cardinal impulse so suddenly that we tend to be taken by surprise, and the trim craft on which we were peacefully sailing through life takes a battering in the turbulent eddies.

Prior to reaching the cardinal cusps (1, 4, 7, 10) shown in figure 1.2.4, we usually can not respond fully to the new type of energy since, in general, we have a passive, waiting attitude and are less inclined to strenuous activity. The reason being that a cardinal axis is always preceded by a mutable house, concerned not so much with doing as with understanding and reflection. Suddenly the action-oriented main axis begins to work in a way that is out of keeping with the more contemplative mutable house. This creates oppositions which we must overcome in spite of an inner reluctance.

The periods before a cardinal cusp are fraught with difficulty. In extreme cases, we may collapse under the burden of duties.

Figure 1.2.4. Cardinal, or angular, cusps.

Frequently there are warning signals in the form of stress symptoms and mild exhaustion. We are plagued by doubts and think, "I can't go on, everythng is getting on top of me." There is a desire to resign, to let everything drop and to cease to bother with anything. However, this is not possible, since so many obligations or self-chosen tasks need our attention. We have to summon up our last reserves of strength in order (like the mountaineer) to reach the top. This demands great exertion with accompanying anxiety states, tensions or a sense of cramping; and yet there is no giving up, no way back—only forward.

Succedent and cadent cusps

Similar considerations apply to the other house cusps, although to a lesser degree. The cross to which a house belongs is always decisive. Before the *fixed* axes of the succedent houses (2, 5, 8, 11), life usually becomes less hectic, but also more stereotyped and unadventurous. Whatever the case, the thrusting cardinal energy is on the wane; in the fixed houses we have to create a fixed form.

Before the *mutable* axes of the cadent houses (3, 6, 9, 12) we are still in fixed houses; usually we seem to be incapable of fitting in to new or changed circumstances. Often our attitude needs to undergo a radical change.

While on the subject of transiting the axes, we should mention that as each cusp is approached, special care ought to be taken to find out how to handle the inflow of new energies and to master the increased demands.

● Rule 4: Advance Influences of the Planets upon Sign Entry

Another rule of interpretation for the correct employment of Age Progression is the following:

> *The qualities or problems associated with a certain planet do not remain in abeyance until the planet is transited by the AP, but come into play as soon as the AP enters the sign in which the said planet is posited.*

Frequent are the passages into new signs which evoke clear and important changes and, in many instances, the latter are attributable

Figure 1.2.5. Planets in the tenth house will begin to act as soon as the Age Point enters the sign of Capricorn in this chart.

to direct planetary contact. It is as if the planets within a sign make their influences felt as soon as the sign is entered. (See figure 1.2.5.) A good analogy is coming into a room already occupied by a number of people. As soon as we walk inside the door we become aware of those present and take in everybody at a glance; we then proceed to greet them individually. The same thing happens when the Age Point enters a sign in which important planets are located. We immediately sense that we have encountered something essential to our development. We do not know just what this is or what it has to teach us, however, as it is only as the AP makes conjunction with the planets that we learn the details.

● Rule 5: Signs Without Low Points

It happens from time to time that a sign is so placed in the house system that there is no Low Point in it. Instead, we generally find a house cusp in the middle of the said sign. Therefore throughout the native's life the sign in question is *axially active* and is correspondingly conducive to success during the passage of the Age Point through it. The curve of success usually rises sharply as the sign is entered and normally remains on a high level for several years. When we find transits through axis-active signs in our charts, we may permit ourselves to take a few risks during this period, as they are fairly certain to prove profitable. Our activities tend to be

Figure 1.2.6. An example chart indicating a Low Point free period in life because of the placement of the signs Cancer and Capricorn in the tenth and fourth houses.

rewarded, according to the nature of the house, more generously than usual. For instance, with the AP in the fourth house there is success in collective matters, in the tenth house we achieve public recognition, in the seventh house our partnerships flourish, and so on. Our example will make this clearer.

In figure 1.2.6, Capricorn and Cancer are both axis-active and also "Low-Point free." In the third house, just after the Low Point at 28° Sagittarius), the AP enters Capricorn, and the IC (at 12°55′) is near the strongest point in the sign.[2] The transit through Capricorn lasts until shortly before the Low Point of the fourth house at about

---

[2]See *The Astrological Houses* for instructions if you don't understand this.

1° Aquarius. A similar situation occurs in Cancer at the opposite side of the chart. Thus only those signs can be termed axis-active which enclose no Low Points at either end.

● Rule 6: Signs with Two House Cusps

If the sign traversed by the Age Point contains two house cusps (as Cancer and Capricorn do in figure 1.2.7), the indications are for an intense and active life-period when the environment brings its influence to bear on us. We may feel overburdened, easily tired or

Figure 1.2.7. Cancer and Capricorn both contain two house cusps in this chart, indicating an intense and active period when transited by the Age Point.

even exploited, since it is hard for us to avoid the claims made on us by the world around. Whatever we take in hand we have to keep working on. The period is full of incident according to the sign, house, or planet concerned and is certainly not a restful one. We may feel that no one is showing us any consideration; everybody seems to believe that we have inexhaustible reserves of energy. Now between the house cusps there is a Low Point signalling recuperation, repair and reorientation, but the claims of the outside world run counter to our needs in this respect: we long for rest, yet are compelled to exert ourselves. In houses like this it is not easy to take proper advantage of the Low Point and often the native is assailed by great weariness. One should adopt a very positive attitude during such periods and should avoid stirring up any unnecessary inner resistance. We shall be helped in our own development if we can work closely with those around us and profit by the stimulus they offer.

● Rule 7: Intercepted Signs

If there are signs with two cusps in them in a chart, there will also be two cuspless signs in it, the one facing the other (see figure 1.2.7). They are known as intercepted signs. The period represented by the progression of the Age Point through these signs is frequently experienced as a resting phase succeeding a particularly hectic period. Resistance to the impulse to take things easy will give us the feeling that we are "running on the spot" and failing to make progress. Our mood can become one of deep dissatisfaction, robbing life of its pleasures and often impairing our health. We become introverted at such times, much as we do when experiencing Low Points. If we picture the Age Point as a locomotive running along a track, we can see that intercepted signs are like sections of track without "points." Therefore the energies cannot be switched to a line running clear out into the outside world, so to speak, but loop further into the inner life via the Low Point. Our impulses cannot escape without a great deal of trouble and we tend to be misunderstood, ignored or unsuccessful. However, if we employ this period to recruit our energies or to reorientate our thinking, we may learn to understand ourselves better—our inner motivation and approach to life.

● Rule 8: Passages of the AP Through an Empty Space

In many charts there are empty spaces unoccupied by planets. (See figure 1.2.8.) As long ago as 1940, the so-called "minor aspect configurations" started to become increasingly frequent. In the forties we were still finding the green quincunx aspects of 150°, but oppositions had disappeared. Between 1982 and 1985, especially in the autumn and winter months, the aspects will be so small that the sextile will be the largest of them. When the planets are bunched, the correspondingly large empty space in the chart creates a sense of uncertainty, or even of helplessness, in the native. The empty space nearly always creates anxiety over the contents of the unoccupied signs and houses. Its vacuum tends to suck in those things that are

Figure 1.2.8. Passage of the Age Point through empty space in the chart.

deficient or strange automatically and, at times, threateningly. One the one hand, there is an increased capacity for finding out and integrating those things that are lacking, while on the other hand there is an unhappy sense of being at the mercy of external influences. The empty spaces are unprotected and allow the entry of all sorts of influences, in fact, especially when the Age Point is moving through them.

If, for example, the aspects are clustered in the upper, "consciousness" part of the horoscope, there are no transits of planets to affect the native until middle life—his forty-third year in figure 1.2.8. Most people seem to come awake only when the AP makes contact with a planet for the first time. They themselves say that until then they have "been asleep." Life has just been lived or, to express it more accurately, has been lived from indefinable motives. Often no outstanding events have marked childhood, and those that have been in any way memorable have been linked with oppositions between the AP and the planets in the upper hemisphere of the chart. Nevertheless, life begins to be lived consciously only when the AP enters the aspect configuration.

Should the planetary cluster be in the lower hemisphere, the AP will exit from it as it enters the upper hemisphere. If the last planet in the aspect configuration stands at the DC, for instance, the significant event will occur at the age of thirty-six. In this case, the Age Point has already transited all the planets during its passage through the first quadrants. The individuals concerned usually undergo many experiences in their early years. Life has been lived very intensely by them, usually in the context of the family or of the profession or of the struggle for existence. When they leave the configuration behind them, they have a more peaceful time in front of them, and they are able to enjoy the fruit of their labors. The empty space does not mean that nothing more will happen; it means that what has already been gained may be improved at leisure, whether the acquisitions in question are inner or outer values. Further information on this point will be found on page 71 in the chapter on the AP Cycle in the Four Quadrants.

● Rule 9: Aspect gaps

Nearly all aspect structures exhibit bigger or smaller gaps, and these have to be taken into consideration. This may be a matter of two planets out of aspect, or of gaps between two aspect configurations. Even when the latter are superimposed or indirectly connected, we react more or less sensitively at the Age Point transits the aspect holes.

Distance halving: turning points

On reaching the midpoint of a gap between two planets or two aspect configurations, we find ourselves at the so-called turning point of the different force-effects. We are leaving the sphere of influence of the first planet (or aspect configuration) and are entering that of the second. Understandably, a change of this sort will be reflected in the life. Where two distinct aspect configurations are involved, there may be a striking change in the native's destiny. Perhaps an example will make this clearer (see figure 1.2.9).

In the aspect picture of this individual, we find in the YOU sphere a gap between Venus and Jupiter. The native reaches the turning point just before the DC when about thirty-five years old. Six different relationships of the Age Point have to be studied in combination for a true appreciation of the significance of its position here. These are:

1. Occupation of the open YOU sphere;
2. Proximity to the sign-change from Sagittarius to Capricorn;
3. Effect of the shadow of the angular seventh cusp;
4. Departure from the unconscious hemisphere and from the lower aspect configuration;
5. Entry into the upper, conscious hemisphere of the horoscope;
6. Position at the turning point between Venus and Jupiter.

Example Analysis

The gaps in the aspect configuration in figure 1.2.9 coincide with the sixth and seventh houses. It coincide with the YOU sphere, which extends here right into the center. Generally speaking, and especially during the period represented by the transit of the Age Point, encounters, contacts and relationships affect people with aspect gaps in this position very intensely. They find it hard to avoid

Figure 1.2.9. Turning points in the "you" sphere at age thirty-five.

them or to guard themselves from any adverse effects. An over-exposed YOU-sphere can signify a close-knit relationship with one's opposite number and much uncertainty and vulnerability in respect of everyone else. Since there is a permanent breach on the YOU-ward side of the native's defenses, he feels endangered by all those with whom he has any dealings. He may see he needs someone to help him keep the rest of the world at bay. Maybe he will look for some strong and capable woman to take him under her protection, preferring to accept her discipline than to fend for himself. If not, he will need to gain mental toughness through spiritual development. Ordinary defense mechanisms are of little use, even though his Mars/Jupiter opposition might suggest that he could resort to attack as the best form of defense—it is better for him to try to understand the fundamental lessons of the aspect gap in his chart.

Since the problem is one of relationships, this man will have to learn to overcome his nervousness and to approach others in an open-hearted way. This he can do only from his center, where love itself protects him and saves him from being so easily hurt. He should cultivate inner strength and independence (Capricorn/Sagittarius) and harmlessness at the Center (or soul).

The *sign-change* is between the mutable fire sign Sagittarus and the cardinal earth sign Capricorn. These individualistic signs have to do with maturation of the personality—mainly in connection with the partner in this particular case. Sagittarius is embedded in the unconscious region and therefore the striving after a more aware spiritual autonomy is as yet ill-defined, and sentimental values and collective thought-patterns are the order of the day (Venus square the conjunction of the Sun and Dragon's head near the IC).

Thus in Sagittarius the native has an opportunity to think for himself, to develop a personal point of view and to wean himself from dependence on the group and their way of thinking. In Capricorn he has the chance to put his new-won autonomy to the proof, and to take responsibility for his own words and actions without advice from the community and without referring everything to his partner for her approval. Potentially, he has a chance of learning to look after himself, without relying so much on her, especially if he can find repose at the center of his being. In any event, an intense learning phase is marked by the passage of the AP through the empty space in the chart and by its transit of the *turning point*, an awakening process where intimate personal relationships are concerned. Something stirs in his soul that urges the native to try and see the world through his own eyes instead of through the eyes of his partner. But, remember, the YOU-side of his chart is very much at her mercy, and she is already in charge of him. She will probably react vigorously to turn him back to herself and to tighten the bonds that bind him to her, perhaps becoming less supportive for a while until he gives in to her demands. He may, indeed, long to "get away from it all" in order to gain inner strength. It is in fact a period in which he could be thrown back on his own resources and has the opportunity to learn self-reliance (provided he is not prevented from doing so by a managing wife).

In our sample horoscope, the native is entering the shadow of the DC and will shortly be moving on into the seventh house (the house of partnerships), and further tasks and lessons are being set that are indispensable to the individuation process. The signs in the YOU-sphere are individualistic and frequently cause conflict between the desire for recognition and its real reason. We may conclude from the Sun and Dragon's Head being conjunct near the IC that an unthinking acceptance of collective norms is now yielding to a conscious adaptation to the native's fellows. Not until the AP reaches Capricorn, however, will this begin to affect the partnership. When Capricorn is entered, Jupiter (on cusp 8) is also activated, indicating that a better balance will be achieved in regard to possession and rigid behavior within the relationships. With expansion of consciousness should come a cheerful assumption of enhanced personal responsibility: the Virgo Sun on the IC indicates a motivation to social work, and Saturn in the region of consciousness gives necessary strength and tenacity of purpose.

● Rule 10: Change of Configurations

In figure 1.2.10 on page 32 we see two separate aspect configurations. The bigger aspect configuration consists of a Sun/Mercury/Dragon's Head conjunction in opposition to Neptune with its attendant aspects to Pluto and the Moon. The other is a "near structure" formed between Uranus, a Jupiter/Venus conjunction, and Mars. It overlaps the main figure, but does not form part of it.

The distances between the tips of the intersecting arms of the two configurations are halved like this: the degrees between the two limiting planets (i.e., the planets at the tips of the two intersecting arms in each case) are counted and divided by two. The midpoint between the two planets is called the turning point. In figure 1.2.10 we find six turning points, and these have been marked by arrows. They enable us to date the ages when the native's life branches out in new directions.

Before anything else, we have to understand what the individual aspect configurations signify. The essential meaning of there being *separate* configurations is that we have to consider two (and in other charts sometimes even more) distinct functions, as revealed by the planets distributed in them. In figure 1.2.10, the linear configuration refers mainly to the sexual desires of the native—thanks to the presence of the libido planets Mars and Venus—but the involvement of houses two, ten and five tells us about his attitude toward economic and professional interests as well.

In the second configuration, the placement in the house system and the planets Neptune, Pluto and the Moon forming the base of the aspect pattern, point to idealistic aims and motivations. What is more, the three leading planets (Sun, Moon and Saturn) are implicated. This has to do with self-realization and with the realization of ideal images of the future. As the Dragon's Head (the Moon's north node) is placed in the eleventh house, aims are fulfilled, especially through friendships, congenial companionship and humanitarian undertakings.

At the *turning points* life is often radically altered, as one constellation and its functions takes over from another. The Age

Figure 1.2.10. A linear structure configuration.

Point is our clue here. In the present example the native is male. At his *first turning point* (between Uranus and Pluto), when he was fourteen years old, he doted on a young woman older than himself and left home for her. A contributory factor was that, at the transit over Uranus when he was six, his father had run off with another woman and had left him with his mother.

When the AP entered Leo, just before reaching the IC, he returned home to train as a technical draftsman, and graduated when it crossed into Virgo some time during his twenty-third year. Virgo is very compatible with the start of professional life, and because he was conscientious (Saturn being in Virgo on cusp 5) his efforts were crowned with success. When the *second turning point* arrived in his twenty-fifth year, he started his own family and became the father of a son as Mars was being transited. At the *third turning point* when he was twenty-seven, his life changed once more. He obtained an overseas post and went to South Africa for three years. There he was disturbed by the plight of the oppressed Blacks but felt powerless to offer any solution to the problems. However the foundation had been laid for engaging in a more idealistic type of work (Axis 5/11 in the second configuration.).

The next great change may be expected at the age of forty-five when the *fourth turning point* is reached. Since this will occur in the eighth house and in Capricorn, he should then be ready to accept the responsibility for a bigger assignment. An Aries Sun in the eleventh house always needs some ideal, for which it prepares the way and with which it fully identifies. The Sun here is in an intercepted sign and is also close to the Low Point, so that apparently this individual will not be able to realize his true goal in life until the age represented by the *fifth turning point*. An intercepted Low-Point Sun invariably takes longer on the road to self-realization than does a Sun on a house cusp.

The significance of secondary aspecting in configurational changes

It is not only the turning points which are the springs of action, but also the change in aspecting from one configuration to another. Figure 1.2.11 on page 34 shows two aspect configurations. The smaller configuration, through which the AP aspects since 1979 run, tends to make the native hyper-sensitive and intent on making harmonious contacts due to the influence of Venus, Neptune, the

Moon and the Moon's node. With Venus on the AC, the reactions can be frankly opportunist, so that the appearance of being a lovable person can be kept up.

From January 3, 1982, the AP aspects have left this configuration to enter the larger one. The last aspect to a planet in the smaller configuration was the trine to Neptune on January 22, 1981; also signalling a "Low-Point year" in the ninth house (Low Point on December 17, 1981).

Since the beginning of the transit of the secondary aspects through the "soft" configuration, starting with the trine to Venus on June 25, 1979, Kohl was thrown on the defensive: Strauss won the

Figure 1.2.11. The horoscope of Helmut Kohl, born on April 3, 1930, at 06.30h, in Ludwigshafen, W. Germany. He became Chancellor of West Germany in 1982.

battle for selection as candidate for Chancellor, giving Kohl time to forge his plans during his "Low-Point year" of electoral defeat.

Subsequently, when the final aspect in the soft configuration was reached (a trine to the Moon's node) he became active again, and organized insidious agitation against the Government (from January 1982).

The main configuration in Helmut Kohl's chart is governed chiefly by the Ego-planets Saturn and the Sun. He gained the ability, thanks to the planets, to the prominence of the cardinal signs and to the T-cross anchored on the main axes, to engage in a compensatory power struggle with extraordinary energy. The AP aspects began to relate to this configuration from January 3, 1982, and when the native was chosen as West German Chancellor, the AP had reached the "minor golden mean" of the vacant space between the configurations. It is hardly surprising that Helmut Kohl became Chancellor, since this new configuration, which is now "ignited" by the AP, gives him an altogether different look. He can assert himself much more forcefully and successfully as Chancellor. The first aspect in this group (a square to Uranus), occurred at the end of May 1984 and at the beginning of June he finally reached his Saturn.[3] Herr Kohl could not have had better timing for a take-over of power.

• Rule 11: Passage of the AP Through Heavily Tenanted Houses

As we follow the course of the Age Point through the chart, houses heavily tenanted by planets are exceptionally significant for interpretation. In figure 1.2.12 on page 36 we see a bunching of planets in the eighth house. Obviously the center of gravity of the horoscope lies here.

Where there is a close-packed grouping of planets, it may be taken for granted that even in his youth the native will consciously experience the simple, physical facets of the area of life (and house) concerned, and that in middle age he will be well acquainted with its theme and concentrate more and more on its spiritual aspects, especially when the "immaterial" planets Neptune, Pluto, and Uranus come to play an important part. In this chart, Uranus and

---

[3] The German edition was published in 1983, so these dates are now in the past. *Tr.*

Pluto form to some extent the framework of the great conjunction in the eighth house.

In order to interpret the passage of the Age Point correctly, we must first be clear about this heavy tenanting of the house and, simultaneously, of Leo. We already know that the eighth house has to do with social structure and with the tendency to protect possessions, status, position and indeed anything owned which could be lost.

Now Leo is a fixed sign, and therefore the struggle for security is partly devoted to the individual's ego, his image, and his intimate sphere. From a psychological point of view, the planetary bunching in Leo in the house of dying and becoming demands the transformation of selfish ambitions into a recognition of the claims of YOU, *i.e.*, of other people and of objective reality. Self-glorification (Leo) is unacceptable to the rest of humanity and has to

Figure 1.2.12. The Age Point passage through a heavily tenanted house means a really significant period in life.

be alchemized in the athanor of the eighth house. Pluto, the planet of transmutation, at the Low Point of house eight demands sublimation of the will to higher, spiritual motives.

With the transit of the Age Point through the eighth house between the forty-second and forty-eighth birthdays, the native will be moved to take a hard look at the established structures, the well-worn systems and the crystallized forms both of the eighth house and of Leo; that is to say both at his own set ways and at those of the community. He will have to decide whether the traditional ways and achievements of the past are still viable and worthy of support, or are a hindrance to further growth and in need of being discarded. Personal desires will have to take second place to the welfare of others, and the individual will have to learn to strike a proper balance between his own aspirations and the justifiable claims of society. There lies the significance of this constellation.

A concentration of planets in one house shows that considerable experience will be gained during life in regard to the matters ruled by the house in question. With the eighth house there is a great readiness to make changes, and changes are regarded as a normal part of life. The sign Leo inclines the native to find his own limits, to mark them out, and then to overstep them! It is a fixed sign in a fixed house, so that development will always go hand in hand with crises and the fight to maintain self-control. The heavily tenanted eighth house provides the equipment for this. Uranus stands on the house cusp and points to a scientific interest in discovering and testing the limits of endurance of self and of others, and in effecting structural and other changes.

An aspect gap exists between Uranus and the Jupiter/Venus conjunction. It is transited in the forty-third year and marks a turning point in life. The native will have to experiment less with his own and other people's resources in the interests of sensible and responsible utilization of his acquired capabilities. Jupiter and Venus come into play and, with their responsiveness to whatever is genuinely true and harmonious, emphasize all constructive aspects. Next to them are found the Sun, Mars, Mercury and Pluto, strewn as it were like seeds of undreamed-of powers now ready to sprout and blossom. The Sun and Mars are experienced as strength, as a compressed ball of energy, mobilizing the internal and external forces and bursting the bounds of the ego. The native will have to emerge from his shell and show who he is, what he can do, and what he has learned in life. The mask so readily assumed by the "Lion" has to be put away so that the true expression of his inner forces may be seen.

During the period represented by the eighth house, this individual will have a golden opportunity to step out of the wings of self, to walk onto the center of the world's stage and to "give it everything he's got." Whether this will turn out more to his own benefit or to the benefit of others will be decided at the transit over Pluto, which as the outermost member of the great conjunction acts as a guardian. In other words, at the age of forty-six, the personal ideal can be reached with the help of Pluto, and the motive-shifting can be completed. It will now be seen whether the native will identify with a nobler goal in life or will abandon his ideals in favor of material ends and of personal aggrandizement.

● Rule 12: Cycles in Tandem with Transiting and Progressed Planets

In this chapter we want to discuss the interplay between the traditional astrological progressions and the Age Point cycle. The way to use the traditional methods is fully explained in various astrological treatises, which it should be quite easy for the reader to acquire, but reference should also be made to the section on "Differences between Age Progression and Other Progression Methods," pp. 10 ff. in *Life Clock*, Vol. 1.

Planetary transits

For transits, the current positions of the planets are taken; their coordinates are looked up in the ephemeris for the time in question and their aspects to the planets in the natal chart are calculated. Long experience has shown that, in this connnection, the slow-moving planets Saturn, Uranus, Neptune and Pluto have a more noticeable effect than the quick-moving planets Mercury, Venus, Mars and Jupiter. Transiting planets either transit their own places in the natal chart or make aspects to the other planets. We have found that as far as Age Progression is concerned the only transits which are effective are those which happen to be in agreement with the theme of the Age Point. Actually, there are two types of agreement: one where the theme of the transit is the same as that of the Age Point, and one where the theme is related.

Identity of theme

This means that the same planet or the same house is concerned in the transit and in the movement of the Age Point. Three possibilities can be distinguished here, as explained by the following examples:

Example A

Let us assume that, in a natal chart, the Age Point has reached the place of the Moon. At this time, which may last for from three to four months, the emotional pole of the native is sensitized and consciously experienced. All transits or progressions affecting the Moon during the said period are felt particularly clearly, since they are in tune with the stimulation of the Moon by the Age Point. Now, while the Age Point is in conjunction with the natal Moon, the transiting Moon (which makes a complete circuit of the zodiac in 28-29 days) crosses the Sun two or three times. From what we have seen, the person concerned is easily irritated on such days, and is apt to lose his temper. There is nothing very significant about this, except that is does enable us to recognize the connection between the AP and the transiting planets. With the quick-moving Moon, transits are more frequent than with any other planet, and so we can observe them more often. Usually a person may not react to such fleeting transits; but when these are supported by an Age Point conjunction with the Moon the entire feeling nature is often thrown into turmoil. There is more on this topic in the chapter on the AP aspects to the ten planets.

Another example would be when the Age Point makes an aspect to Saturn, and transiting Saturn simultaneously crosses the Ascendant or some other strongly emphasized place in the chart. The effect of Saturn on the Ascendant is intensified due to the stimulus of its Age Point aspect.

Example B

Somewhat different is the case when the Age Point and a transiting .planet simultaneously aspect one another and a third planet in the natal horoscope. If, for instance, transiting Jupiter makes a square aspect to the Age Point, nothing much happens; but if both Jupiter and the Age Point jointly aspect a third element, the effect is felt. *General Rule:* Only a triangular relationship between the transiting planet, the AP and the radical planet will have any detectable effect on the native. Linear relationships do not seem to work.

Example C

A further possibility for theme identity is when the Age Point is in the same house and in the same sign as a transiting planet. Say the Age Point is in the sixth house in the vicinity of the Low Point, and transiting Jupiter is on the cusp of the sixth house and aspecting a planet in another house at the Low Point. Transiting Jupiter will be strongly felt and we shall also experience the contrast between Low Point and cusp.

Theme identity might also be illustrated when, for example, transiting Uranus passes over the radical Sun as well as the Age Point. A feeling of unrest is experienced, but not more so than when only the Age Point passes over the Sun. It is the same phenomenon that one has observed when the Sun and the Ascendant occupy the same sign: the intensity of the sign's effect is not doubled but on the contrary, weakened. In the case where Uranus transits the Sun, Uranus can, however, serve as a timer when there is a time interval between the conjunctions of the AP and of transiting Uranus to the Sun. We do not perceive the conclusive action of the AP/Sun conjunction until the moment when Uranus passes over it—and this can occur one or two months earlier or later.

Relatedness of theme

This occurs either when the transit is in the same house as the one currently occupied by the Age Point, or when it makes aspects with planets also aspected by the Age Point. The following examples should help to elucidate this:

Example A

If, say, transiting Saturn reaches the place of Mars in the radix in a house which is also occupied by the Age Point, then its effect will be definitely felt. However, if the Age Point is not present in the house in question, the transit will pass without trace. Here is the reason why so many predictions made from planetary transits fail to materialize. Experience goes to show that the slow-moving planets have a more pronounced effect on our development when they are able to make common cause with the house theme as activated by the Age Point. Therefore, the Age Point enables us to get our bearings both as to the sphere in life and as to the age level of the person concerned, whenever we are studying his situation with the help of transits.

Example B

Relatedness of theme also occurs among the planets themselves. In figure 1.3.4 on page 55, the planets have been arranged in three columns according to the Huber Method. Column one contains the female planets, Venus, Saturn and Uranus. Column three contains the male planets, Mars, the Sun and Pluto. And colume two contains the neuter planets, Mercury, Jupiter, the Moon and Neptune. So if the Age Point is conjunct the Sun at the same time as transiting Pluto makes an aspect with Mars, the native's self-awareness will be challenged and activated. All three male planets have a common theme: self-assertion, decisiveness, self-control, etc. Should the conjunction of the Age Point and the Moon coincide with an aspect from transiting Neptune to Jupiter, the capacity for love and affection will be increased not only by the AP aspect itself but also by the theme-related transit.

Progressed planets

By these we understand the planetary positions on the days after birth as given in the ephemeris. Their motions are interpreted by the rule: "A day for a year." The aspects made to each radical place during these "day-years" are then studied.

Interest centers mainly on the quick-moving planets—the Sun, Moon, Mercury, Venus, Mars and Jupiter—and how their influence is strengthened by Age Point aspects to radical positions. The Moon's directions are especially liable to stir up emotional conditions when the Age Point happens to be aspecting the Moon.

Table 1. List of Planetary Correspondences with the Age Point

Age	AP Cycles in Relation to Planets
Age 6	AP at cusp 2, tr. Jupiter in opposition to radical Jupiter.
Age 12	AP at cusp 3, first return of Jupiter to its radical position.
Age 18	AP at cusp 4 (IC), tr. Jupiter in opposition to radical Jupiter.
Age 22	AP at Low Point of 4th House; tr. Saturn square radical Saturn.
Age 24	AP cusp 5; second return of Jupiter to its own place in the radix.
Age 28	AP at Low Point of 5th house; tr. Uranus trine radical Uranus, tr. Neptune sextile radical Neptune.
Age 29½	AP coming up to cusp 6; tr. Saturn conjunct radical Saturn.
Age 30	AP at cusp 6; tr. Jupiter in opposition to radical Jupiter.
Age 36	AP at cusp 7; third return of Jupiter to its radical place.
Age 38	AP at IP in house 7; the Dragon's Head reaches its own place in the radix for the second time.
Age 42	AP at cusp 8; tr. Uranus in opposition to radical Uranus; tr. Jupiter in opposition to radical Jupiter; tr. Neptune square radical Neptune.
Age 48	AP at cusp 9; fourth return of Jupiter to its own place.
Age 52	AP at Low Point in house 9; tr. Saturn square radical Saturn.
Age 55	AP separating from MC; the progressed Moon reaches its own place in the radix for the second time; tr. Uranus trine radical Uranus, tr. Neptune trine radical Neptune.
Age 56	AP at IP of 10th house; Dragon's Head reaches its radical place for the third time.
Age 60	AP at cusp 11; tr. Jupiter conjunct radical Jupiter (for the 5th time).
Age 72	AP at the Ascendant; tr. Jupiter conjunct radical Jupiter (for 6th time).

Table 1: Continued.

Age	AP Cycles in Relation to Planets
Age 82	AP at Low Point of 2nd house; progressed Moon conjunct radical Moon; tr. Saturn square radical Saturn.
Age 83-84	AP approaching cusp 3; tr. Uranus conjunct radical Uranus; tr. Jupiter conjunct radical Jupiter, tr. Neptune in opposition to radical Neptune.

AP cycles in relation to transits and progressed planets

On considering the transits and progressions of planets, we observe an interesting relationship to Age Progression. The stages of life as defined by Age Progression receive surprising confirmation from transits and secondary directions. Transits taken out of context can create a false impression. The interconnections between the orbits of all the planets in the solar system and the bearing of these on the various stages of life are described by Alexander Ruperti in his book *Cycles of Becoming.*[4]

Since we are dealing here with the concerted action of many elements, we shall review them chronologically as shown in Table 1. We shall designate the planetary positions in the natal horoscope as "radix" or radical positions. The only progressions we have included are those of the Moon.

In figure 1.2.13 on page 44, the correspondence of the transit cycles of the slow-moving planets and of the Dragon's Head with the Age Point is shown. In constructing this diagram, we used the average values of all respective revolutions of the planets in our own century, because the main intention is to offer something which can be usefully employed for persons alive today. If a study is being made of famous individuals of past centuries, allowance will have to be made for deviations in timing.

In the case of Pluto, the deviations are considerable in our own century also: its speed has doubled since 1900. Therefore we have drawn the topmost line in three variants, showing its real

---

[4]Alexander Ruperti, *Cycles of Becoming*, CRCS Publications, Reno, NV, 1978.

Figure 1.2.13. Correspondence of the transit of the slow-moving planets and Dragon's Head with the Age Point. At the bottom of the chart the years are indicated, with special prominence given to cuspal Age Points (6, 12, 18, 24, etc.) and Low Points (4, 10, 16, 22, etc.). The actual houses are given underneath. The upper lines display the transits of the slow-moving planets on the same time-scale. The prolonged transits of these planets to their radical places are shown. Where the more recently discovered planets are concerned, all the aspects in the thirty-degree series are listed. With Saturn, for the sake of clarity, we have confined ourselves to four positions: the ascending square/opposition, and descending square/conjunction. With Jupiter and the Dragon's Head, only the opposition and the conjunction are given. The numbers in the symbols representing the latter mean "revolutions." Thus, 1 = first revolution, 2 = second revolution, and so on.

● Conjunction   ⚹ Sextile   ▲ Trine   ⚻ Quincunx   O Opposition

⚺ Semisextile   ■ Square   ⚼ Semisextile

movements (not the averages) for people born in 1900, 1930 and 1960. In neighboring years the pattern is similar. The considerable differences for those born earlier or later are evident; the distances between the aspects become shorter and shorter (e.g., lines 1 and 3 in figure 1.2.13).

Several interesting patterns emerge on closer inspection, such as, for example, the almost exact coincidence of Jupiter's returns to its own place (in 11.96 years) with the passage of the AP over alternate house cusps.

As compared with this, the rhythm of Uranus and Neptune takes the form of an octave of seven intervals, and this overlaps the AP and Jupiter only at the ages of 42 and 84. Thus Neptune's ascending square, the first opposition of Uranus and the fourth opposition of Jupiter to their own places, all occur in the forty-second year of life just before the Age Point transits cusp eight.

The other planets do not follow either the six-year or the seven-year rhythm, but help to highlight important stations of the Age Point. Thus Saturn's first descending square occurs shortly after the passage of the AP through LP 4 (separation from the parents), etc. We shall have to leave it to the reader to find further interesting "meshing points" (there are many more!).

Chapter 3

Age Point Aspects

AP activity and its evaluation—Rules governing aspect activity—Rules for finding the AP aspects—List giving sequence of aspects—Duration of the AP aspect activity—The natures of the planets—Feminine, masculine and neutral planets—Hard and soft planets—Aspects by color—Triggering a configuration—Planets void of course—The comprehensive approach—Aspect interpretation in three stages—Planetary tables—The aspect cycles of the AP—Primary aspects of the AP—Conjunctions—Oppositions—Beginning of the full cycle—The two semi-cycles—Five intermediate stages—First semi-cycle—Second semi-cycle—General rules for the sequence of the aspects—Primary aspects in childhood—Hints on interpretation—Beginning of the AP cycle in the four quadrants—Three kinds of aspect—Red aspects: conjunction, opposition and square—Blue aspects: sextile and trine—Green aspects: semisextile and quincunx—Three development stages in the quincunx aspect.

• AP Activity and Its Evaluation

In Age Progression we use only the seven classical aspects (see figure 1.3.1 on page 48), by which is meant all aspects of thirty degrees or multiples thereof, including of course the zero degree, (0°, 30°, 60°, 90°, 120°, 150°, 180°); the conjunction (0°) and the opposition (180°) being the most powerful—for which reason they are termed the primary aspects. All other angular relationships, such as the semi-square, sesqui-square, quintile etc. are not considered. Nor is any notice taken of the ill-conceived division into good and

Semisextile 30°	Quincunx 150°
Sextile 60°	Trine 120°
Square 90°	Opposition 180°
Conjunction 0°	

Figure 1.3.1. The seven principal aspects in a horoscope. When we use colors to indicate aspects, we draw them in as follows: green for the semisextile and quincunx, blue for sextiles and trines, red for squares and oppositions, and orange for conjunctions.

bad aspects, which unfortunately is still made at times, even today. The evasive reformulation of "bad" and "difficult" or "hard" and of "good" and "easy" or "soft," had been rejected also. Such terms as good and bad are inapplicable to the Age Point, too, because this evaluation a) is useless from a psychological point of view; b) is not applicable to the individual in his developmental phases; c) does not take into account that in Age Progression the aspects work differently from the way they work in classical astrology; d) ignores the concern with inner experiences rather than with outer events.

In astrological psychology we are interested in the development of the inner person and not with what is going to happen next (or with good luck and bad luck). The method of interpretation and, indeed, the effect of the aspects, both differ from what we would expect in the traditional modes of prognosis. What is more, Age Progression deals with an internal clock, timing mental and spiritual processes—not happenings in the physical world, although there is of course a functional relationship between the inner and the outer. "Why and wherefore" is more important than "what" in Age Point aspects because the crux of the matter is self-knowledge.

Since the Age Point position is the focus of our present consciousness (see Vol. 1, p. 46), the way the aspects operate depends very largely on our conscious attitudes. How we react to the stimulus provided by the AP and its aspects is the decisive factor: everything depends on whether we are prepared to come to grips with what the inner selectivity draws (so to speak) into our orbit from outside, or whether we are more inclined to shirk the challenge.

Finally, it is we ourselves who decide if an AP aspect has a positive or negative effect on us. Often we find that the so-called good or easy aspects create more problems than do the bad or hard ones. The latter can have an extraordinarily helpful effect on our psychic development.

Rules governing aspect activity

Another essential difference from traditional methods of prediction is that in Age Progression the only events indicated by aspects are those having some subjective content; events, in other words, making a deep and lasting impression on the mind. Such impressions are made when the archetype corresponding to the currently aspecting planet is activated in our psyche, and our own creative power provokes or selects (as the case may be) the experience necessary to our development. The Age Point represents the everpresent consciousness, which moves through time "zipping together" the inner and the outer life at each moment.

For astrology, each planet represents one of the ten basic properties of mankind. In the course of life, these are stimulated, made active, and brought into consciousness by the Age Point aspecting the planets in the horoscope and we become acutely aware of the planetary qualities. If we are sensible, we will come to terms with it and will learn how to make best use of the tools or weapons with which we are furnished at that time. Nevertheless, the matter is a personal one and it is difficult, if not impossible, to lay down rules for the influence of the aspects.

It is advisable to ask oneself, "Is the experience which I am trying to associate with the Age Point one which has been significant for me, causing me considerable concern and presenting me with a challenge, or is it one I have been able to live through without problem?" Quite often we undergo sensational experiences which leave no trace behind them; others of apparently no significance may almost swamp us in their wake. It is our subjective evaluation of them which matters: everything depends on what they mean to us. The fact that a person nearly always places a subjective construction on whatever happens to him is a psychological truism. Accordingly, only those experiences stamp themselves on the mind which touch our inner being; they, only, are registered by the Age Point, and the latter fails to respond to what is purely objective. Perhaps the following examples will help to put these ideas into perspective.

When a mother dies after several years of illness, one would imagine that the exact time of her death would be revealed by the Age Point. Yet this is not inevitable. Say that, owing to the terminal nature of the disease, the native had become resigned to the loss of his parent several years before it happened; it is this psychological event and not the death itself which is signposted. Again, in cases of separation and divorce, events will often cast their shadows before, even though the partners may stay together for several years longer. And the reverse can also be true if a decision is forced upon the native. Therefore, the exact date when the decree is made final is not so relevant. Many a time we fail to notice the commencement of a new cycle or process of inner changes; we do not see how our attitudes and reactions are being subtly remodelled. Then sudden external circumstances may reveal that something has taken place within us that we may have consciously or unconsciously refused to face in the past. Hence there is little sense in compiling a list of events with which to test the Age Progression method, unless those events have been deeply experienced. The Age Point indicates solely those things that have changed us.

Rules for finding the AP aspects

As we know, astrological aspects are specific angular distances between individual planets. Frequently in a chart we find two or more planets so close together that we can say they are in conjunction (0°). When the Age Point reaches the radical position of a planet, this too is regarded as a conjunction. We then refer to the AP transiting a planet. If the AP confronts the planet across the chart, at a distance of 180° measured round the 360° zodiac, then it is in *opposition*. They are the two most important, or *primary*, aspects as far as the Age Point is concened. However, five further aspects are formed between the extremes of conjunction and opposition: 30° (semisextile), 60° (sextile), 90° (square), 120° (trine) and 150° (quincunx). These are the seven classical aspects already mentioned by Ptolemy.

Example

For aspect-finding practice, we shall look at the 1983 position of the Age Point in figure 1.3.2. on page 52. In this year the native is forty-one years old. The AP has reached 25° Aquarius and makes a semisextile with the Moon (at 24°09′ Pisces) and shortly afterwards a quincunx with Neptune (at 28°18′ Virgo). When he attains the age of forty-eight, the AP is on the ninth cusp and comes into conjunction with the Moon and, almost simultaneously, into opposition to Neptune.

For beginners, an aspect-finder may prove useful. With its zero marker placed over the Age Point, the aspects can be read directly. Naturally, the appropriate orb is allowed for the AP and for the planet concerned. Advanced students can easily recognize the aspects without any aids however.

In temperate zones, the transit of a sign by the Age Point can take anything between three and twelve years, and the rapidity of aspect formation with each planet varies accordingly.

Figure 1.3.2. Example chart calculated for May 10, 1942, Zurich, Switzerland. The planets are arranged according to *degree number* (irrespective of sign) below the chart. The Age Point always follows the same order of the planets in making the various aspects, and aspects them (potentially) once per sign.

The natal chart really reveals an individual pattern of response linked with time, a pattern that remains the same throughout the native's life. As already mentioned, however, the time spent by the AP in the various signs can differ considerably. Hence in a large house (embracing more than a sign) the aspects may follow one another quickly (many experiences). For example, during the six-year transit of a house all the planets can be aspected twice (making 20 or more aspects in 6 years when a house covers more than 60°).

By way of contrast, in a small house the AP "creeps" over the degrees of the zodiac contained in it. So perhaps no more than three, four or five aspects are formed within 6 years. Nevertheless the poverty of aspects is compensated by the intensity of experience (see also Vol. 1, p. 62).

This phenomenon evokes different responses in people of different types. For instance, someone with a more static personality (with strong occupation of fixed signs and/or houses; several squares) can be "overrun" by the activity going on in a big house. A flood of sensations, together with unsettled feelings, inhibitions, and anxiety in the face of responsibility can result. A dynamic personality (with emphasis on cardinal and mutable signs and/or houses; aspects of the triangular or linear type) may find time hanging heavy on his hands during a slow period, *i.e.* in small houses. Restriction or paralysis, lack of success, lack of drive, and introspective or depressive phases may frequently be explained by this phenomenon, especially when such reactions are atypical.

Duration of the AP aspect activity

In analyzing the Age Point aspects, care must be taken that the so-called *time orb* is observed (see Vol. 1, p. 57). It goes without saying that this can be expressed in degrees, according to the house size. However, since in the Age Point we are dealing with temporal measurement, it is expedient to express the extent of the activity in terms of time. The duration of an aspect is longest in the case of conjunctions and oppositions—the main AP aspects, and the effective influence (the time orb) is often in the region of a year. When the Age Point comes into conjunction or opposition with an ego-planet (Sun, Moon, Saturn) or occupies some other significant place in the aspect structure (a center of tension, or a stellium), the following points should receive due consideration:

Figure 1.3.3. An example of planet activity upon entering a sign.

1. The aspect activity begins with a conjunction and an opposition upon entry of the sign, in which one or more planets stand, regardless of whether the first degrees of the sign are before or behind a cusp. (See figure 1.3.3.)

2. The activity becomes more intense as the planet is approached and quite often reaches its high point on the very day the aspect is exact.

3. A clear cessation of the effect is observed—if not immediately, then within two or three months following the transit. In other types of aspect the orb is naturally smaller. On average, 1° before and after the exact aspect is the orb in a 30° house. If the house is small, the orb is smaller too—sometimes only ½ degree; if the house is large, the orb before and after the aspect place can be anything up to 2°.

● The Nature of the Planets

Generally speaking, in the aspects there is a reciprocal action between the different planetary principles. In judging the aspects, attention should be paid (both in radix and Age Progression) to the natures of the planets involved; so it will be useful, at this stage, to discuss one or two planetary categories:

Feminine, masculine and neutral planets

From this division it is easy to determine whether the qualities of planets are in tune or not. Take a look at figure 1.3.4 and

Spiritual Growth: Super-Conscious Sphere

Creative Intelligence	Love Ideals	Spiritual Self
♅	♆	♇
Uranus: Meditation; Method or System	Neptune: Identification; Understanding; Empathy	Pluto: Contemplation; Metamorphosis; Growth

Personality (Ego): Conscious Sphere

Physical Manifestation	Feeling of Identity	Self-Awareness
♄	☽	☉
Saturn: Practical Thinking; Need for Protection	Moon: Sympathy; Need for Contacts	Sun: Will; Need for Expansion

Life-Supporting Functions: Subconscious Sphere

Perfection	Formulation/ Evaluation	Achievement/ Efficiency
♀	☿ ♃	♂
Venus: Assimilation; Longing for Harmony	Mercury/Jupiter: Media Sense; Learning Capacity	Mars: Motor Action; Energy

Figure 1.3.4. The nature of the planets.

you will find three columns showing which planets have related qualities and which have not. The planets on the left side, that is to say Venus, Saturn and Uranus, we shall treat as feminine; Mars, Sun and Pluto on the right side, we shall treat as masculine; Mercury, Jupiter, the Moon and Neptune are counted as neutral. Planets in the same column are related in quality and motivation and supplement or support one another, even though they can differ considerably in their reactions and functions. Planets taken from different columns contradict one another when in aspect, causing problems and tensions.

Hard and soft planets

A further distinction has to be made in reading the aspects, and that is between soft (sensitive) and hard (purposive) planets. From this it is possible to tell whether certain planets harmonize in their basic qualities or not. The *soft, sensitive planets* are the Moon, Mercury, Venus and Neptune, and to some extent Saturn (depending on sign and house potential). The *hard, purposive planets* are the Sun, Mars, Saturn, Uranus and Pluto, and to some extent Jupiter.

Effect of the AP aspects on sensitive planets

Sensitive planets team up well with blue and green aspects since their natures are similar to the latter. But these planets often begin to make their presence felt for the first time under the influence of red aspects, because the latter activate the planets more vigorously. Frequently, however, such aspects behave as irritants, and cause exaggerated behavior and hypersensitivity. What is significant, of course, is whether the native develops in keeping with the Age Point, or raises resistance to inner or outer change—which might change the effect accordingly.

Effect of the AP aspects on purposive planets

Purposive planets react exceptionally strongly to red aspects because the natures of planets and aspects are similarly forceful. The planets' energies are activated and changes are produced in the outside world. Green and blue aspects, on the other hand, act as irritants on hard planets; they often make the native uneasy and indecisive. Many people fail to react to them at all.

● Aspects by Color

We have color-coded the aspects in order to make classification possible. The colors orange, red, blue and green have been adopted from a color-psychology scheme as follows:

Conjunction—Orange—Power
Compressed, creative force is expressed by this color. Note, however, that according to the qualities of the planets a conjunction can also be "red" or "blue." The deciding factor is whether hard or soft planets are involved.

Opposition and square—Red—Energy
This color has been chosen because it corresponds to the energy and its realization as found in these aspects. These are the aspects of Action.

Trine and sextile—Blue—Matter
These are the aspects which have a peaceful, relaxing quality. They are the aspects of Matter, or rather of Feeling.

Quincunx and semisextile—Green—Consciousness
These are seeking, informational, often undecided, too; they are the aspects of thought and perception.

We shall study the aspect colors in more detail later, but at this point would like to introduce the reader to a further rule to be used in judging the Age Point aspects: first of all determine the type of aspect(s)—red, blue or green—made by the planet in the radix. For example, when the relationships are only *green-blue*, then the reaction to red AP aspects is very strong. The expansion of consciousness receives a big impetus with the input of a force that was not previously there.

The same sort of thing happens when a planet has only *green-red* aspects. If it receives a blue aspect from the AP, the capacity for relaxation and enjoyment is improved, which is all to the good in this tense type of aspect formation.

Finally, if the planet's aspects in the radix are *red-blue* and it receives a green aspect from the AP, the ambivalence inherent in the polarization into energy and feeling (red and blue) can be handled with greater awareness. The prevailing either-or attitude is toned down and the individual becomes more tolerant and wiser, because he can perceive the intermediate shades.

● Triggering a Configuration

The next important rule for a psychological elucidation of the aspects is never to confine attention to single aspects but to consider the total configuration at all times. On comparatively few occasions do we have to do with individual planets or aspects where the Age Point is involved. Usually the Age Point triggers a whole aspect figure. Therefore we should determine which planets in a configuration are touched in rapid succcession. Only in this way can we obtain an accurate idea of which tasks still await accomplishment and of which problems can now be solved.

● Planets Void of Course

The Age Point will often cross a planet that is aspect-free; this is full of importance, because hidden or latent qualities are then brought into the open. The period is one of experimentation and of gathering experience. Each Age Point aspect represents a fresh opportunity to experience something new through the planet in question, to observe the non-integrated factor in one's reactions and improve one's self-knowledge step by step. A conscientious observation of oneself is imperative. A transit of the Age Point can be an enriching experience or, on the other hand, a source of vexation. Our friends may find it difficult to understand why we suddenly do something entirely out of character.

● The Comprehensive Approach

In astrological psychology we are well aware that in order to comprehend the native, we have to study his horoscope as a whole. Excessive concentration on details will lead to error, as experience has shown; alas, the pitfall is often hard to avoid! It can hardly be emphasized enough that we gain most help for our development from the Age Progression Method when we keep the total aspect picture in view—which should not be too onerous a task if the mode of representation used in this book is adopted. Observe how the aspect configuration is neatly delineated in the chart in red, blue and green. From this it is easy to pick out various geometrical figures: big, all-embracing triangles, small triangles, quadrilaterals and straight lines.

● Aspect Interpretation in Three Stages

As we have seen, a number of different factors have to be taken into account in judging the aspects. The best course is to proceed as follows:

1. First determine the house in which the Age Point is currently placed. For a differential diagnosis of the possibilities, note whether the AP is in the beginning, middle or end of the house (see The Age Point and the Intensity Curve, Vol 1, p. 49).

2. Next identify the sign involved and, once again, note whether the AP is situated in its beginning, middle, or end.

3. Finally see whether any of the planets in the house are being approached closely by the Age Point, calculate when the conjunction is exact, and find out what other aspects to individual planets or to the whole aspect configuration are being made.

When we have learned to combine these three elements satisfactorily, we shall be in a position to assess the effects of the aspects with accuracy.

The sequence of the different Age Point aspects can be seen as a temporally ordered whole when it is considered from the standpoint of a history of development. In seventy-two years each planet goes through one entire aspect cycle of the Age Point. This cycle consists of two half-cycles (one ascending and the other descending), of thirty-six years each. Only the seven main aspects are used, and successive aspects represent successive stages in the native's development (see figure 1.3.1 on page 48). The following rules have to be observed:

1. In order to trace the development of the capability indicated by a given planet in a given position (house, sign, aspect), the Age Point aspects must be seen not in isolation but as stations along a cyclic

track through the whole chart—and, by extension, through the whole life.

2. An aspect cycle begins with the *first primary contact* of a planet (conjunction or opposition). During a half-cycle, the Age Point runs in thirty-six years to the opposite place in the chart; taking a further thirty-six years during the second half-cycle to return to its starting position. But in seventy-two years we experience only *one* half-cycle as a unit. The other is divided into two widely separated time periods by the beginning-cum-end of life (the AC).

3. The self-contained half-cycle invariably starts in the first half of life, with either a conjunction or an opposition with or to the planet concerned, all depending on the sector of the chart in which the planet stands. With planets below the horizon we begin with the conjunction (ascending cycle), with planets above the horizon we begin with the opposition (descending cycle).

4. *Sign aspects.* In every sign, the AP makes an aspect of one sort or another with the various planets. When, for example, a planet is 18° Scorpio, the aspects always fall due at the eighteenth degree of each sign. When a planet is 5° Sagittarius, we have to inspect the aspects made at the fifth degrees of each sign as the AP travels through the zodiac.

5. *House aspects.* The Age Point activates the planets not only in the signs but also in the houses. As it transits the cusps or Low Points of the several houses, it triggers planets on cusps or Low Points in the radix. Once again, the dynamics of development are in seven stages, and understanding should be gained through introspection. Such aspects produce no spectacular effects, but do have a subliminal action that is valuable for our spiritual development.

• Primary Aspects of the Age Point

Figure 1.3.5 shows that the aspect cycle commences either with a conjunction or an opposition to some radical planet. Therefore these two aspects are the most important of those made by the Age Point. They are known as the primary aspects and usually elicit unequivocal, powerful effects which boost our development. Being formative factors of the first rank, they mould our characters—but in such a way as to cause traumas and complexes if the planet in question is poorly placed.

Aspects preceding the start of the aspect cycle are preparatory; so to speak setting the scene. The actual performance does not open until direct contact is made with a planet, and the particular branch of drama to which it belongs is decided by whether the ascending or the descending half-cycle is being entered. In practice we can distinguish the following effects:

a) *Active effect* (Conjunction): This occurs in all conjunctions where planets are situated in the lower part of the chart. Say a planet stands at the third cusp, the cycle will then commence in the twelfth year of life and will reach the opposition thirty-six years later when the native is forty-eight, after the first half-cycle has been completed. During this period the specific influence of the planet is stimulated until it reaches consciousness.

b) *Passive effect* (Opposition): This is produced when the aspect cycle starts with an opposition, *i.e.*, when the planets occupy the third and fourth quadrants. During the passage of the AP through the empty lower houses the native is mainly subject to the influence of his environment; a state of affairs over which he has little control. He is quite likely to repress some of the contents of his mind, even to the extent of amnesia: events and experiences being often forgotten unless they have been impressed on the native for some reson or other by parents or educators, especially when they occurred early in life. The conjucntion and opposition of the Age Point will now be examined in greater detail.

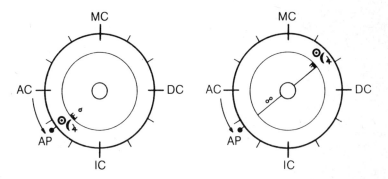

Figure 1.3.5. The primary Age Point aspects are the conjunction and opposition.

Conjunction of the AP

Whenever the Age Point makes a conjunction with a planet, the latter's basic influence emerges into full consciousness. The planet is experienced quite intensively and at close range. It gives us no peace; we have to keep paying it attention to find out what it means for us. The best approach is one of positive, even welcoming, acceptance. Putting the matter a little quaintly, we might say that the planet conjunct the AP lies right under our nose, and there is no possibility of stepping back to see how wide and deep its influence goes—no way either of taking the bearings of the attendant problems, because we are too much involved in them. At such times the unknown is liable to fill us with dread. The more we attempt to avoid a confrontation (either through fear or ignorance) with the principle represented by the planet in question, the more we are likely to be confronted with it by fate—perhaps in a drastic fashion. It depends on the planets and their aspects in the birth chart whether it is in youth or in adulthood that conjunction aspect cycles start. As for the planets in the upper part of the chart, something is learned about their effects when the AP makes an opposition with them, long before it reaches their conjunction. Coping with them at the time of conjunction is therefore so much easier.

At all events, it is the significance of a conjunction that we identify ourselves with the life-force concerned and note in actual experience what the planet does in us, what qualities it promotes, and which functions it performs in our lives. During the conjunction, which lasts for several months, we learn most about the planet. Therefore we should take advantage of the opportunity and undertake a conscious exploration of its relationships. By so doing we shall learn more, more quickly, and shall move on to maturity. Five additional aspects lead up to the opposition, which marks the end of assimilation and development and indicates the time when we can take stock of what the learning process has had to teach and of where it has led us.

Opposition of the AP

Matters are different where the opposition is concerned. Not only is it true that when a conjunction has preceded the opposition we do not have the same situation as when AP contact is being made for the first time, but also, in either case, we now find ourselves at some distance from the planet as we ride along with the Age Point; hence we are unable to identify with the planet fully. On the credit side, everything to do with it is spread out before us as in a panorama: its other aspects, its position in house and sign, and its neighboring planets. We are able to see its interconnection with the rest of our environment and to gain insight into the psychological and spiritual background. A disadvantage is that the opposition can easily throw us into a passive, defensive position. Over against us, on the opposite side, so many things are happening out of reach of our direct control. Nevertheless, the resultant tension does have a considerable teaching effect: we start to see how various factors in our lives hang together, and we understand the meaning and purpose of the learning process—which is worth a great deal! Consciousness is expanded and so is self-assurance. If the aspect cycle commenced with a conjunction and the AP has already transited the planet, everything the planet has to offer is now available to the conscious mind. With the opposition we reach what might be called a peak, and what we require are maturity, responsibility and deliberation. Before us lies the *phase of realization*, which opens the way to greater freedom.

● Beginning of the Whole Cycle

As already mentioned, the AP moves once around the entire chart in seventy-two years, aspecting each planet as it goes. Depending on house position, the AP can come into contact with a planet very early in life (if the first quadrant is occupied), or perhaps not until the native is middle aged. Whatever the case, the technical rules remain the same, but for the purposes of psychological interpretation, due regard must be paid to the age of the native when the planetary organ (capacity) begins to develop. There are certain relevant questions:

1. Is the planet above or below the horizon in the radix? If below, the causes for the subsequent development of the capacity are unconscious; if above, they are conscious.

2. In which quadrant is the planet? In other words, at what age does the aspect cycle commence? We shall have more to say about this later.

3. In which half-cycle do we currently find ourselves? If in the ascending, we are fully occupied developing the planetary quality, but if descending, we can put it to good use in our life.

The two half-cycles

The full tour of the chart is divided into two parts. The first runs from conjunction to opposition and lasts thirty-six years; the other returns from opposition to conjunction and also lasts thirty-six years. Figure 1.3.6 shows how we start with the conjunction of the AP with a planet and make five other aspects before reaching

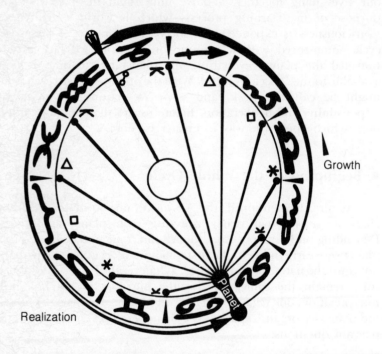

Figure 1.3.6. The Age Point aspect cycles. We have called the ascending AP *growth* and the descending AP cycle *realization*. The ascending cycle starts when the AP is conjunct the planet concerned, wherever the latter may be in the chart; the descending cycle starts with the opposition, *i.e.*, when the AP faces the planet across the chart. The individual stages are the seven classical aspects (each separated by 30° from its neighbor), marked by their respective symbols.

their opposition. This is a process of mental growth and provides an opportunity for learning and gaining competence in some special ability. After opposition, the road back to conjunction is characterized by a process of practical application, and realization.

The time has now come to speak in more detail of the *secondary aspects*, which make five stages between the two *primary aspects* in each half-cycle. There are five of these.

The five intermediate stages

These five intermediate stages, or secondary aspects, are the semisextile, sextile, square, trine and quincunx—taken either in this or in the reverse order for either of the half-cycles concerned. The interpretation of these aspects depends on whether the half-cycle is ascending or descending. For example, we can say that a square in the ascending half-cycle strongly stimulates the desire to reach a goal, whereas in the descending half-cycle it stimulates the urge to make good and active use of what had already been acquired.

The following cycle of aspects is presented so that the principle we shall now discuss can be well understood.

First Half-cycle
(the ascending one in this instance)

Conjunction of the AP (0° angle): Let us suppose, for the sake of simplicity, that a certain planet is standing on the Ascendant. (See figure 1.3.7.) Here the AP conjunction is present at birth, and the given influence begins to unfold right away. There can be no question of a conscious perception of such subtle qualities in infancy; planets on the Ascendant frequently point to a traumatic birth (see also page 117).

Growth

Figure 1.3.7. An ascending half-cycle.

Semisextile of the AP (30° angle): Some six years later (the exact time depends on the size of the house) there is a semisextile to the planet. In our example, this happens at a very early age, but perhaps even at this age the native had a dim inkling of the nature of the planetary influence on him or her. There is a certain amount of repetition, usually as the native becomes aware of the more obvious consequences of the conjunction. Basically, the semisextile is a mercurial aspect, relating to the field of information. Circumstances come into our lives which compel us to cope with each of the planetary influences. Many a time we learn by our mistakes.

Sextile of the AP (60° angle): Some six years later again, when the native is twelve years old, he or she enjoys the feeling of having come to terms with the planetary influence concerned; having had the first taste of success in overcoming certain problems connected with it. A hope arises in the mind that the individual's objectives have already been gained.

Square of the AP (90° angle): But then, six years further on, at the age of eighteen, the square produces a crisis. Everything seemed to be nice and safe during the sextile period, but now comes the "crunch" when the native must prove his or her command of the situation. Wrong judgments, absurd behavior and illusions will often arise from the conscious mind in response to external stimuli. It turns out that the planetary influence has not yet been fully understood, and the more rashly the native jumped to conclusions during the sextile period, the heavier is the reckoning now. More intensive work is required to elucidate the qualities symbolized by the planet. But since a fresh surge of energy accompanies this Martian aspect, the native will be able to set to work with a will. The square is the most important aspect next to the conjunction and the opposition, because it represents the midpoint, and therefore the crisis point, between the two main aspects.

Trine of the AP (120° angle): In another six years the AP reaches the trine to that planet with which the cycle began. The planetary capacities have ripened slowly and are now in full bloom. Everything comes relatively easy and there are a few genuine triumphs. Subjectively, a sense of optimism infuses the native when applying the resources of the trined planet. Smugness and pride are the danger, and the native may think there is no need to do anything more; yet, much more is on offer, even from the point of view of worldly achievement, than has so far been suspected.

Quincunx of the AP (150° angle): At the age of thirty or thereabouts the effect of the quincunx is felt, encouraging new and (this time) spiritual aims. An unknown world, stretching out in a spiritual dimension, can suddenly break in and change the life. Here is the start of a wider program of perception and learning, often linked with decisions of crucial importance. The abilities are applied to fresh goals in life. The quincunx has deep significance in Age Progression: it plays the most direct part in building consciousness, with the Age Point representing as it does the focus of the native's consciousness in time and space. When we come to describe the green aspects we shall have more to say on this.

Opposition of the AP (180° angle): The opposition is reached just thirty-six years after the conjunction. There are two possibilities here. If the native has failed to cultivate the abilities represented by the planet, the opposition may herald collapse, presaged by a certain feeling of helplessness during the quincunx aspect. If, however, the proper adjustment has been made at the time of the quincunx, concrete opportunities of which the native has not yet dreamed will open up at the opposition. The opposition can create extraordinarily favorable situations, since we have swung out to the greatest possible distance from the planet in question and can look at it in all its bearings.

The Second Half-cycle
(descending in this case)

Now comes the second half-cycle of thirty-six years, covering the same aspects (in reverse order) back to conjunction. (See figure 1.3.8.) Just as the first thirty-six years relate to growth so do the second thirty-six years relate to the realization of what has been developed. The faculties can now be put to good use in the outside world. Disintegration will occur only if the opposition has not been mastered and the native has remained immature and infantile.

Once more a part is played by the five intermediate aspects in making practical applications easier for the native to handle. Naturally, these aspects do not have quite the same significance they

Figure 1.3.8. A descending half-cycle.

had in the first period, inasmuch as stages of manifestation are not the same as stages of growth.

The ascending and descending movement may be compared to the life of a plant, which begins with a seed buried in the earth. We could say that the seedling breaks the surface at the semi-sextile and sprouts up until it reaches its first flowering at the sextile. The blossoms are beautiful but have to give way to the start of fruiting, corresponding to the square aspect. At the trine the fruit are fully ripe, and at the quincunx we find out whether they are sound or rotten. Come opposition the fruit are picked, and during the second half-cycle they are enjoyed and digested. What is more, in the first phase the plant grows toward the sky into a spiritual dimension, while in the second phase its forces return to the soil. In the negative sense there is a process of dissolution and death, in the positive a process of manifestation. Like everything else in Age Progression, this development depends on whether or not the individual concerned perceives the laws of growth within himself or herself and wants to live by them. It is the quality of consciousness that decides. In those who still have no concept of personal freedom and responsibility, the Age Point aspects have either a negative effect or none at all. The descending process during the second half-cycle then takes a negative course (i.e., one that is distressing and bound up with mental suffering) if the opposition has ushered in a collapse. In, on the other hand, a positive second phase the benefits gained can be consolidated.

• General Rules Governing the Sequence of Aspects

Only with planets on the Ascendant does the Age Point take an "ideal" course. Its journey can begin at any stage in the aspect cycle, but it will have to wait until it comes to a conjunction or opposition before the influence of a planet is fully felt. As already said, the AP aspects which precede a conjunction or an opposition have a preparatory effect.

The native does not yet feel directly involved, and can wait unperturbed until the conjunction is reached. Say, for example, we have the first effective contact with a planet as shown in figure 1.3.9 where there is an opposition to ninth-house Saturn from the third house at some age between twelve and eighteen as the AP transits the third house. Two aspects have already been formed since birth, a trine and then a quincunx. In general, these would represent a foretaste of something which will not become fully established until later. The experiences associated with them are divorced from practical matters, because the native cannot yet see how they apply to himself or herself. Therefore they leave no imprint on the character. This is the province of the primary contact when it comes. Where planets are close to the CD, this conjunction that makes such a clear impression on the character will not occur until the thirty-sixth year of life. Where the planets are in the twelfth house, the first primary aspect takes place at opposition when the AP is in the sixth house. In these two last-mentioned instances all five secondary aspects have already been made and have laid the groundwork for what is to follow.

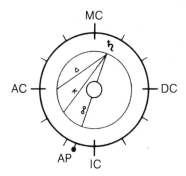

Figure 1.3.9. The Age Point in opposition to radical Saturn indicates the first effective contact between AP and Saturn between the ages of 12 and 18 years (third house).

• Primary Aspects in Childhood

In planets placed just after the AC or DC (see figure 1.3.10), primary aspects occur as early as the first or second year of life in either case. The effects are often traumatic. Since the child is as yet unable to have any conscious say in what is going on, he is completely at the mercy of the planetary influences. Taking this approach, we can read the formative events and traumas of childhood from the chart by tracing the course of the first quadrant from the AC to the IC. The first eighteen years of life may be taken as character-forming in general, although in some individuals the process is completed earlier while in others it lasts until the Age Point is well clear of the IC. During this period the native is strongly influenced and moulded by his environment. The character, which later arises from this, bears the stamp of the circumstances of youth in many respects. All oppositions and conjunctions in these first eighteen years serve to "bend the twig that will later grow into a tree." Whenever there are planets in the first and third quadrants, we have influences in the early years requiring careful investigation. (We shall return to this point later.)

It ought not to need saying that these impressions must not be regarded as inherently negative, although in the event of traumas there can often be severe inhibitions. By traumas we mean every character-forming experience of a planetary quality that leaves behind a strong impression which is hard to shake off, because the native feels he was a prey to circumstances. Circumstances can also throw up some special talent which then becomes fully active.

Figure 1.3.10. Traumatic aspects involving the Age Point and a radical planet may have long lasting effects.

Hints on interpretation

In interpreting youthful impressions, we have to run a check on the intensity of the conditioning, with due regard to whether or not the native has any freedom of awareness (age!), as well as considering his degree of dependence on his environment—whether he lives passively in the control of mother or nurse, say, or strives to develop interests and opinions of his own. As soon as this is known, we usually find a logical and straightforward interpretation of the native's problems or of his so-called compensations. Always there is that which is obvious or that which is concealed. The best thing to do is to ask the person concerned about what he has experienced. The rule is this: the person who compensates reacts unconsciously, the person who meets conflicts head-on reacts consciously. Thus whoever has suffered under hard primary aspects (and remembers his sufferings) has in some measure come to terms with them and is ready for further growth. But whoever compensates, that is to say suppresses problems and projects them into the world (laying the blame for them on others), is tormented by complexes or unconscious fears and behaves differently from what the planetary situations require. In instances like the latter there is often a very imperfect recollection of childhood. Before matters can be put right, a genuine effort must be made by the native to uncover the causes of his wrong attitude. True healing of a so-called disorder has to start with the uncovering of its root. In many cases this will require psychoanalysis.

• Beginning of the AP Cycle in the Four Quadrants

It will now be useful to see what happens when the aspect cycle begins in other regions of the chart. When the AP transits a planet that is not on the Ascendant (but in some other house position), the aspect sequence may begin with a secondary aspect. Alternatively, the process may start with an opposition should there be one or more planets in the third quadrant; in which case, the AP moves through the five minor aspects until it reaches the conjunction. Either way we have the same process of the perception, growth and realization of a capability. To recapitulate once more: at conjunction the half-cycle of construction begins, and at opposition the half-cycle of exploitation. The native's maturity in terms of age will naturally have to be taken into account when an analysis is made. All this will now be explained by dividing the chart into its four quadrants and looking at each in turn.

Quadrant 1: When the first contact (shown in figure 1.3.11) made by the Age Point to a planet takes place in the first quadrant, there is a corresponding process of growth in early life, even without any contribution from the infant consciousness. It goes without saying that external formative forces will be more influential in the first three houses (at ages 0-18 years) than in the later ones. In the former, the human psyche is still weak and unformed, and reacts with great sensitivity to seemingly insignificant events. There is no mature ego and therefore no properly aware response to the conjunction of Age Point and planet. Nevertheless, a powerful confrontation does take place with the planetary principle. If the planet concerned is an ego planet (Sun, Moon, Saturn), it is still not possible to handle it properly or to integrate the activated self-consciousness (the Sun) into the life. Attendant problems will not be finally solved until the opposition arrives. In the course of the aspect cycle the same set of themes is encountered at each stage (each aspect). By the time of opposition (after thirty instructional years) the problem and any traumas should have been overcome.

Quadrant 2: When a planet is standing in the second quadrant (see figure 1.3.12) life starts in the descending phase. Although the native profits by experience (perhaps gained in a former existence?), it is not until the conjunction of the AP with the planet concerned—at some age between eighteen and thirty-six—that he realizes that so far

Figure 1.3.11. Age 0-18. The first, second and third houses.

Figure 1.3.12. Age 18-36. The fourth, fifth and sixth houses.

he has not correctly understood or consciously mastered the planetary influence, even though behaving as if he had done so. The time of transit brings the first distinct awareness that much yet remains in the planetary position, and a new learning process begins. In the ascending cycle of trying and testing, the influence is brought more into consciousness; at the opposition, after thirty-six years, the native has managed to come to terms with the whole complex issue and can explore all its possibilities. Thanks to the wealth of experience acquired, the native is on a higher curve in the spiral of development, which then begins again at the conjunction (at an older age or perhaps in the next life?).

Quadrant 3: Figure 1.3.13 on page 74 illusrates the Age Point starting in the constructive half-cycle at a period in which the native's mind has been enriched by experience. Having passed through the minor aspects, he can apply some practical wisdom to the planet. His developmental phase began with an AP opposition in the first quadrant in youth. Nevertheless, the conjunction itself is not an end, but the beginning of a new process of learning and experience, usually at a more aware and at a higher level—by which we mean that the spiritual side of a planetary quality is promoted where possible. The individual who closes his mind at this point and assumes that he has no need for more experience and growth, because he already knows everything, will either be forced to develop further by inner or outer crises or be left stagnating. And stagnation is followed by resignation and senility, in that order. A conjunction of the Age Point with a primary principle requires the native to venture into new areas of experience. The planets enter with their

Figure 1.3.13. Age 36-54. The seventh, eighth and ninth houses.

full archetypal power into his consciousness and demand attention and promote participation in what is going on.

Quadrant 4: Figure 1.3.14 illustrates the hardest position—planets in the fourth quadrant; the native is then plunged into the building-up process at birth. A semisextile, sextile or square would be the first aspect encountered; therefore, root contact with the planetary influence is lacking—the native will attempt to deal with it this way and that and will be no more than semi-successful until the time of opposition when he knows what is really at stake. In the end he will see the planet in proper perspective against its background. From the vantage point of the opposition, he will be able to make a general survey of the planet's relationship to see how it functions. Although the native may previously (and for much of his life) gain insight in the sense of understanding into this planetary quality, he will not be able to use it much by way of development. It is too remote. People with many planets in the fourth quadrant are mainly "late developers."

Figure 1.3.14. Age 54-72. The tenth, eleventh and twelfth houses.

Figure 1.3.15. A second beginning

Only between the ages of fifty-four and seventy-two, when the AP comes into conjunction with one of the planets, can the latter be genuinely experienced in its deepest quality—generally through understanding. When the fourth quadrant is reached, "being" rather than "doing" is what matters. And so the fruit of past endeavors is usually "not of this world."

A Second Beginning in the First Quadrant: In figure 1.3.15 we see there is a chance that the native will be confronted with the influence of a planet he has encountered before, but on a higher turn of the spiral. He is now in a position to review past experiences, the childhood impressions and traumas. Perhaps he will discover the deepest meaning of the successes and failures, the joys and sorrows which have fallen to his lot. Even if he can no longer take a very active part in life during what is now a second ascending half-cycle, the seed is already being sown for the life to come. Should the native survive to the second transit of his first-quadrant planets, he can discover entirely new dimensions in them—the shores, so to speak, of other worlds. This is the great virtue of survival to an advanced age.

● Three Types of Aspect

It makes it easier to explain the aspects if we divide them into three types, which can be labelled with the colors red, blue and green. We will term the red aspects energy aspects, the blue aspects matter aspects, and the green aspects consciousness aspects.

Red Aspects

Conjunction: ♂
Opposition: 180° ♂
Square: 90° □

The red aspects (see figure 1.3.16) are invariably the expression of an inner dynamism, vitality, or motor energy. When the Age Point makes a red aspect with a planet, new forces are released in us in keeping with the planet concerned. Even the so-called "soft" planets (i.e., Moon, Mercury, Venus, Jupiter), have their functions intensified by red aspects. They release energetic processes in us and, often in our surroundings, too, thus bringing about the most significant changes in our manner of life.

The red aspects affect our attitudes rather than our readiness to do something positive. They act on the way we operate, not on our inner nature as the blue aspects do. For this reason we have to respond actively to such aspects; they give us an opportunity to overcome the fears and inhibitions which have so far held us back. Now we can rid ourselves of outworn conditions, either in our circumstances, in our occupations, or in ourselves. At the same time we must be prepared for possible conflicts with those around us, since any changes we make will frequently meet with their opposition. Fortunately, red aspects bestow the necessary courage to deal with the opposers.

However, if we allow ourselves to be beaten, and fail to do what needs to be done, the period can be one of suffering. And so the red aspects are classed as negative in traditional astrology. The native may willingly put up with suffering, may take excessive strain, when he ought to be reacting differently. He feels, perhaps, an

Figure 1.3.16. Red aspects: conjunction, opposition, square.

unaccountable disinclination to settle down to the work he should be doing and, because this gives him a sense of guilt, he engages in all kinds of hectic, but pointless, alternative activities. His strength is wasted—with nothing much to show for it. What is more, hastiness and a lack of proper control easily entail errors. How tempting then to say, "The red aspect has done this to me. Obviously, it is a bad aspect!" On second thought, however, the honest native would be compelled to add, "It was my fault, too. I jibbed at the challenge."

Where the red aspects are concerned, it is particularly important to determine what they require of us. The aspected planets should be closely studied to see at what points the personality needs refining. Then new actions can be broached intelligently, consciously and placidly, and positive results can be obtained in keeping with the nature of the planets concerned.

Further Rules of Interpretation for Red Aspects

Naturally, red aspects to the "hard" planets (Sun, Mars, Saturn, Uranus, Pluto) have a more powerful effect, since the planets and the aspects have much in common. Depending on the nature of the aspects in the natal chart, problems can become intensified. The individual either tends to become obdurate, or, in the best cases, to become confirmed in his essential strengths. Given the right approach, the same aspects can lead to putting one's abilities to work for the benefit of others, especially when they involve the spiritual planets (Uranus, Neptune and Pluto). A strain that would be too great for one person can prove to be an incentive to development for another—since he will appreciate the need to accept bigger tasks and responsibilities and, by doing so, to resolve his internal conflict.

Conjunction of and Opposition to the Age Point

As we have already mentioned more than once, conjunctions and oppositions are the most powerful of the seven aspects where the Age Point is concerned. Usually their ingress is marked by external events, which can bring about marked changes in behavior and life-style: in negative cases these changes take the form of mental blocks, repressions, depressions, refractoriness and aggression; but in the positive ones the change activates inner powers or the achievement of long-held ambitions—all according to the nature of the planets in question.

The Square to the Age Point

This martian aspect gives a great boost to further development. It activates us more strongly than does the opposition, but makes us more quarrelsome too. We are stirred by lively external and internal forces; and submerged wishes (and also problems, as the case may be) are brought to the surface, according to the planets and aspect configurations involved, and to the house and sign occupied by the AP.

At such times our aims and efforts may meet with opposition, but generally this will only incite us to strive the harder. A square often creates dissatisfaction with existing conditions, making us rebellious and more than ever ready to leap to the defense of our freedom and independence—but making us nervy and irritable, too, perhaps. This is especially true when the AP is aspecting "hard" planets. With aspects to "soft" planets, on the other hand, we have the temptation to intemperance and other excesses. It is not uncommon to find that the square lends a drastic character to what is going on around us.

With leading planets, i.e., those positioned near one of the main axes or standing out strongly in the aspect configuration, the four red aspects formed with each planet by the AP in the course of its travels (conjunction, square, opposition, square) can be clearly recognized during a cycle of circa eighteen years. Now and again they stand out as landmarks in life.

Blue Aspects

Sextile: 60° *
Trine: 120° △

The blue Age Point aspects (see figure 1.3.17) have to do with human "substance." Usually they inaugurate a process of change in our essential qualities. In other words, they rearrange us internally, making a qualitative, and often a quantitative, alteration in our potential. The blue aspects activate and mobilize latent capacities and release them for use. Not only do they envelop and mould us on the outside, they thrust themselves "under our skin" so to speak and

Figure 1.3.17. Blue aspects: sextile and trine.

set to work on making a radical alteration in us whether we will or no.

Because blue aspects penetrate to the roots of our being, it is next to impossible to escape their influence. At times their effects can be quite unpleasant; our bodies are drained of energy and we feel physically ill. And, once their influence pervades us, they will start attacking our ingrained habits and dissolving crystallized conditions. If we have been over-comfortable, have been living with a false sense of security, and are resting on our laurels, we shall have to start giving of ourselves once more. The "softness" of these aspects is deceptive; they can be very demanding. However, what they do to us will depend very largely on the planets being aspected and on the house and sign occupied by the Age Point.

The Sextile to the Age Point

A sextile between the Age Point and a planet will aid the solution of outstanding problems. Sextiles are venusian aspects, for which reason they often foster new relationships and the pleasanter side of life. The native becomes more adaptable and tolerant; he understands people better and can find excuses for their failures. The sextile frequently acts as a modifier and helps him to reach a compromise when involved in any dispute. His esthetic sense is heightened too. But this sense then causes discomfort if it is offended: in other words, depending on planet, sign and house, the native may over-react to petty annoyances, unwelcome events, and anything that is nasty or unpleasant. Having entered a state of harmony, he expects to be left in peace to enjoy it. Often he dreads conflicts and is ever ready to compromise—anything for a quiet life. Also, a type of assimilation process takes place during this Age

Point aspect. Often the time is now available to digest previous experience or to absorb new impressions.

The Trine to the Age Point

When we have acted creatively in some way or other, and have turned to account what certain planets have had to offer, a feeling of happiness rises within us, our reward being some solid achievement to enjoy. We can sit down and rest for a while, in the knowledge of having provided ourselves with a reserve for future needs. A new confidence in living emerges to compensate us for past strains and anxieties.

Yet there is also a risk that we will take things easy for too long and will lose sight of the fact that life is in an eternal state of flux, requiring new adjustments every day. If we have too little solidity about us, our lack will prove painful. All wrongs and errors ought now to be abandoned, so that our affairs can move forward in a happier vein. It should no longer please us to behave as if we were content with everything because a life of constant ease can end in satiety.

Trines may also lead to a continual hunt for perfection and to susceptibility to disease.

Green Aspects

Semisextile: 30° ⊻
Quincunx: 150° ⊼

Green aspects (see figure 1.3.18) act directly on our consciousness. They do not concern our human substance or demand of us any kind of activity or performance. Their effect is to make us wide

Figure 1.3.18. Green aspects: semisextile and quincunx.

awake and more keenly aware of what is going on around us. Through deeper reflection we come to realizations that promote our development. There is no need for our thinking to become rigorously logical at this time; more probably our conscious thought-life will be enriched by hunches and inspirations.

The term just used, "conscious thought-life," is a wider concept than "thinking"; it expresses what comes with the assimilation of all our experiences, and includes not only intellectual activity but sensory perceptions, together with those intuitive feelings that make hidden knowledge accessible to consciousness. Green aspects help us to be sensitive and open to new lines of thought.

Therefore the two green aspects have a special significance for the Age Point, being the main switchboards in our decision-making.

Decision-making possibilities peak during green aspects, by reason of the fact that not only is the Age Point primarily the focus of consciousness, but also these are the aspects which have to do with consciousness and thought. What is more, such aspects in the main promote not external performance but the activities of consciousness: clear thinking, the acquiring of experience, and decision taking. Squares are typical activity-incentive aspects, yet may encourage rashness and so lead to unfortunate results. When the green aspects arrive they help to correct such errors; they aid in the gathering of fresh information, and shed light on complicated situations. Although blue aspects allow scope for an individual's talents they can also lead to plethora and conceit. Green aspects, on the other hand, can make us aware of this fact that sometimes "virtue itself turns vice."

The Semisextile to the Age Point

At the semisextile we become desirous of learning, are eager to enrich our experience at the hand of the planet concerned, and many times commence a regular study of its properties.

When a semisextile is being interpreted, it is important to note whether the aspect is ahead or behind the conjunction. If we are looking at the second half-cycle, with the conjunction coming up, the native is usually absorbed in theory. He is still unsure of himself and is troubled by the notion that his practical knowledge of the quality represented by the planet is still deficient. Only at the following conjunction does he make the necessary identification with it. At the next semisextile (the one coming after the conjunction) it is easier for him to pass on whatever he has learned. He is communicative and keen to hear what others have to say on any subject. Therefore he can be found engaging in exchanges of opinions more frequently than formerly. He is more talkative and inquisitive and more intent on imparting his knowledge to others. As mentioned earlier, the Age Point traces out a continuous learning process, so that the action of one aspect forms a prelude to the next. Only at the opposition do we begin to reap the benefit of everything that is accessible to us through the aspecting planets.

The Quincunx to the Age Point

We would re-emphasize here what has been said before, namely that this aspect has a special significance in Age Point progression. We call the long green aspects the big stride forward in thought by way of contrast to a "little step forward in thought" (the semisextile). The long green aspect often creates uncertainty, due to a proneness on the part of the native to think ahead longingly to some distant goal. Therefore this is also known as the wistful or suspenseful aspect. Once again, it is important to determine whether the aspect comes before or after the opposition. Before the opposition, it is experienced as a yearning after some remote objective. In many instances it begets irresolution and crucial decision-making, and (after a long period of effort, of weighing up the pros and cons, and of looking for answers) can signify an acceptance by the native of the challenge to limit himself to a specific aim. When he does so, however, it will usually be after the opposition has been passed. The effect is to strengthen consciousness and will in keeping with the quality of the Age Point as a focus of consciousness.

• Three Stages in the Development of the AP Quincunx Aspect

There are three stages in the life of the long green aspect: In the first stage, the native is insecure and hovers between various thoughts and desires. He builds castles in the air and projects his innermost wishes on others, or on the far unknown. Without knowing what he really wants, he has the vague feeling that he was born to be a "somebody." He is easily influenced and will usually do just what he is told, gladly being subject to a stronger will—at least until he knows his own mind. He becomes a seeker, and an ill-defined longing drives him on.

In the second stage he is beset by doubts. Although his daydreams still please him, he is troubled by a nagging suspicion that things are not quite right. He now begins to think, to ask questions, to philosophize. A regular Faustian struggle develops with all its intellectual dissatisfaction and crisis of faith. Truth wears many faces for him, and the native sees so many possibilities that he tends to lose himself in the relative. Nothing he can do enables him to decide what is worthless and what worthwhile; he falls into a severe decision crisis.

In the third stage the native recognizes that everything depends on him; he must decide to restrict himself to a single matter, even if this is at the expense of his freedom, his fantasy life, or his ideal picture of himself and the world. Here is where the will is trained. Realizing that he will never achieve everything he would like to do, he settles for something less, even if it is not his first choice. And if he abides by this decision, he can be fairly confident that a day will come when his purpose will be gained and, what is more, that he will be a more resolute, maturer and wiser individual. The long and difficult way is also the way forward. Therefore we call these aspects development aspects.

But there are pitfalls. If the native defers making decisions that would benefit his inner growth, the long green aspect to the Age Point will make itself felt in some outer event corresponding to the planetary nature and will force him to face essentials. In the United States, the quincunx aspect is also known as "the finger of God" because it is often associated with the buffets of fate attendant on irresolution and a lack of sound judgment in the native.

It is wise to prepare for such quincunx aspects in good time—especially where the ego-planets (Sun, Moon and Saturn) are concerned. We must arrive at decisions which will lead to inner growth. What is more, it is important to recognize and, if possible, to solve EGO problems. Then, when the long green aspect arrives, we shall already know what is required of us. This is the very considerable help afforded by a knowledge of Age Progression in the horoscope!

Chapter 4

Age-Point Aspects
to the Ten Planets
and to the Lunar Nodes

Introduction—Age-Point aspects to the three personality planets—The Sun: AP
transit (conjunction)—House position of the Sun—Aspects and aspect-cycle of the
Sun—The Moon: AP transit (conjunction)—House position of the Moon—Aspects
and aspect-cycle of the Moon—Subjectivity—Green aspects from the Moon—Sense of
personal worth (sensitivity)—Contrasts existing in the emotional body—The child
like Moon Ego: spontaneity—Saturn: transit (conjunction)—House position of
Saturn—AP aspects and aspect-cycle of Saturn—Mercury, Mars, Venus, Jupiter: AP
transits and aspect cycles—Uranus, Neptune, Pluto: AP transits and aspect cycles—
The Lunar Nodes: AP transits and aspect cycles

● Introduction

In judging the aspects made by a planet to the Age Point, it is
necessary to refer to the natal chart. We cannot properly assess an
aspect or house position from the Age Point alone; the chart must be
taken as a whole. A planet is found not only in a house and sign but
also in relationships with other planets. All these together impart a
characteristic—and permanent—coloration to the basic influence of
each planet. Potentially this coloration can give lifelong problems,
which are activated from time to time by the Age Point.

In order to evaluate the AP aspects as comprehensively as
possible, we must be systematic and elucidate the following points
in connection with the Age Point and planets:

A) Status of the Age Point:

1. House position of the Age Point;
2. Effect of the house;
3. Stage of life represented by this house;
4. Sign position of the Age Point;
5. Aspect to Age Point (conjunction, semisextile, trine, etc.);
6. Color of aspect (blue, red or green).

B) Status of the Planet:

1. Number of aspects made by planet in the natal chart;
2. Colors of these aspects;
3. Sign position of the planet;
4. Whether planet is strongly or weakly placed in the sign (strongest point 12°, weakest point 0° or 29°);
5. House position of the planet;
6. House region where planet is posited (cusp, invert point, low point, before or after the axis).

In judging an Age-Point aspect we must not assume that the native will make full use of the positive possibilities of the planetary position. When the radical position of the planets has some afflictions, difficulties of various degrees of severity can arise (compulsions, compensations). But this can be established only at an interview. During a counselling session with a client such potential problems have to be taken into consideration and evaluated.

• Age-Point Aspects to the Three Main Planets: Sun, Moon, and Saturn

In the aspects made between the Age Point and the Sun, Moon and Saturn, we see mirrored the development of personality into autonomous individuality. Our point of view is the human EGO anchored in three planes: the Sun representing the mental plane, the Moon the emotional plane, and Saturn the physical plane. The concerted action of the three EGO planets depends on their radical positions. From these we learn how the total personality is constituted and where its strengths and weaknesses lie.

It follows that, taken together, the Age-Point aspects made to the three personality planets are involved with 1) our ego, self-observation and degree of conscious autonomous thought (Sun), 2) our emotional liability and impressionability (Moon), and, 3) our physical safety and things "practical" (Saturn). Attention must always be paid, however, to the house region in which a planet is posited. On the cusp, the planet receives unlimited feedback, that is to say, it receives corroboration from the environment. At the Low Point, on the other hand, it prompts remoter, more uncertain and more subjective reactions. A person with planets at the Low Point is often totally unaware of any feedback. Here we find a distinction that makes it hard to lay down general rules for the AP aspects. In what follows we shall do our best to supply a comprehensive description of the effect of the AP aspects on the main planets; on the other hand, the leading indications only will be mentioned for the other planets.

● The Sun

The Sun is the symbol of the self-conscious mind, and of the logical thinker. Aspects between the Age Point and the Sun present a challenge to autonomous thinking that could lead to self-development. It goes without saying that it will help to increase independence and personal application. Events that support this trend tend to occur.

Transit or Conjunction

At AP-transit, the Ego's mental pole, or "solar" consciousness is activated. Generally, the native has a creative urge and a longing for adventure; he wants to "sit on top of the pile" and attract the attention of others. The Sun bestows the strength and courage to make his own decisions and to go his own way, even at the risk of a certain amount of failure. To enjoy a healthy self-confidence, he needs to trust his own ability and to accept responsibility for himself and others. This gives him more confidence to develop. According to the time of life of the native, and to the sign in which the transit occurs, there is a desire for freedom and self-determination.

House position of the Sun

When the Sun stands in the tenth house, for example, a transit through the fourth house brings us in opposition to it; then we have the strength of mind to make a conscious break with the aims of our community, our parents or other authorities. No longer do we need to wait for confirmation, permission or applause—we can get along under our own steam. On the other hand, when the Sun is actually standing in the fourth house, an AP transit will occur between the ages of eighteen and twenty-four. It is then the meaning of the fourth (not the tenth) house which has to be used in interpreting both Sun position and AP transit.

With a fourth-house Sun, we usually bow to community rules or family tradition whatever our initial objections. We gain in self-confidence by performing household duties or by accepting some function in the community or family.

Since the Sun also symbolizes the father (who is a key figure in the formation of our own self-confidence), it may also come about that—according to the aspects thrown to the Sun in the Radix—our self-confidence is braced or undermined by the father or by some father figure such as an employer of a government department. How this will work out in practice will depend on the situation as a whole, and is not easy to predict in advance. In consultation work, it is best to avoid concrete predictions and even to ask the client how he or she is experiencing this phase.

The aspects and aspect cycle of the Sun

As the solar aspects come and go, the native grows more practiced at using the force of his personality and at recognizing the strengths and weaknesses in his personal development. He can afford to smile indulgently at offers of encouragement and support from those around him and to make his own decisions without reference to anybody. Surprisingly enough, this is accepted by his fellows, even when (owing to a Low-Point position of the Sun in the radix) he himself has the uncomfortable feeling that he is being rather daring with them. In AP aspects to the Sun, the native experiences a greater inner and outer security and freedom in doing whatever he thinks to be right. Solar consciousness is autonomous and does not depend on consent. Independence and self-assurance will tend to be boosted every time an AP aspect is made to the natal Sun.

This theme is modified according to the nature of the aspect. By referring to the aspect cycle and its description, the reader will be able to trace the gradual development of self-confidence and, possibly, of self-realization. As mentioned above, we have to allow for the Sun's radical aspects, since self-consciousness is largely influenced by associated planetary forces. These, too, are activated and brought into play by the Age Point aspects.

Thus with a natal Sun-Mars trine, Mars is co-aspected with the Sun when the Age Point transits the latter. The native then had the chance to show that he is as secure, strong and self-confident, as is indicated in his radix. Again, if the Sun is in conjunction with Venus or Mercury, these will share the transit with the Sun. With Venus, self-confidence will depend on harmonious surroundings, on personal esthetics, and even on whatever panders to the native's vanity. With Mercury, the intellect comes into play and may be brilliant at this time.

The above are no more than a few of the possible combinations. Every serious student of astrology should make sure of being able to define the qualitative effects of the basic planetary functions and should be able to work out their joint influences. (See also *Life Clock*, Vol. 1, p. 194, "Basic Functions of the Ten Planets.")

• The Moon

The Moon has to do with our emotional self, which puts us in immediate touch with our surroundings. Whereas the Sun's Age aspects enhance self-confidence and will-power, the Moon's Age aspects enhance the need for contacts, the capacity for love and sensitivity. In astrology, the planets and other elements of the horoscope may be considered from various points of view. So the Moon can be seen as representing the contactual ego, the juvenile ego or the emotional ego. These are merely different names for the same function, as we shall see. The Moon does not stand for the autonomy of the self as the Sun does, but for the perception of personal emotional responses to our surroundings. Through our relationships with people and with plants and animals, we receive confirmation that we possess a contactual or emotional ego, and that we are sensitive and responsive beings. Self-knowledge of the lunar ego is experienced in the following way: "I am being noticed, I am being understood," or simply, "I am being loved." These feelings are especially noticeable at Age Point conjunction or opposition at which times the heightened sense of personal worth brings happiness.

Human emotions predominately react on themselves, i.e. subjectively. Because of our human egocentricity, they work like a magnifying glass, enlarging all our impressions. But perhaps an even better comparison would be with a fairground "crazy" mirror, seeing that our subjectivity invariably distorts reality either positively or negatively. Egocentricity also provokes rash judgments based on the current situation of the native, so that his one thought is, "This is good and that is bad for me." When the Moon "objectifies" or differentiates, it is into for and against, into sympathy and antipathy.

Transit (conjunction)

On direct transit there is a conscious experience of the emotional ego; usually through a closer knitting of relationships. This closeness is responsible, however, for emotional ups and downs: sympathy and antipathy, attraction and repulsion, can follow one another like ebb and flow.

The lunar conjunction causes an extra strain in our emotional structure; therefore the meaning of the Moon for our development needs to be examined in more detail. At the transit, we become more acutely aware of our personal wishes in respect to contacts, and seek to emerge from any comparative isolation to find satisfaction in proximity to our fellows. Whether or not we really get close to them will depend largely on how the development of our emotional life, as a whole, has been going. Anyway, we find it easier to surmount difficulties in handling others during this period, when we are honest with our feelings, since the Age Point activates all the emotional components relating to the Moon. If, in the meantime, we have suffered or are still suffering from emotional frustrations (a state of affairs frequently indicated by red, and occasionally by green aspects in the radix), this fact will now become painfully apparent.

House position of the Moon

As already mentioned, the interpretation of a transit of the Moon's place has to be guided by house position and by the age and maturity of the native. For instance, if the Moon is in the fifth house, the emotions will be stirred up at the age between twenty-five and thirty, either by some new love affair or by separation. In the fifth house, the Moon will retain a certain tendency to endorse childishness, and to some extent will make the native want to cling to what he already has. His sense of personal worth will depend on whether and on how much he is loved. Every readjustment will arouse jealousy and a struggle for possession; possibly the process of maturation will take place only through some painful loss, some rejection, some defeat in love, or a changed relationship.

Moon aspects and aspect cycles

In essence, there is a development of emotional qualities and values during all AP aspects to the Moon. The improvement of the capacity for making contacts, and for love, occupies the foreground, and frequently we even experience the very things that we need for our development: love won, love lost, and loneliness. Generally speaking the amplitude of the "pendulum swing" ruling this process is considerable, since our emotions are polarized between good and evil, love and hate, joy and sorrow, etc. For this reason the differences between the various aspect types are much easier to trace in Age Point aspects to the Moon than in Age Point aspects to the Sun and planets.

Responding to the qualities of the individual aspects, we work our way through change after change until we acquire emotional stability and become able to solve, with conscious intent, the problems arising from interpersonal relationships. Most folk suffer from emotional problems of one kind or another; but this is all part of being human.

To recapitulate, then, on what to expect from the aspects: Blue aspects bring reassurance and harmony, red aspects nearly always cause a certain amount of commotion, difficulty and hardship, and green aspects engender longings, undefinable states of the feelings and a sense of insecurity.

Green aspects to the Moon

The green aspects promote development through an increased capacity for comprehension. Our maturation is oriented toward the most relaxed and balanced emotional state as possible; for it is only composure and inner harmony that makes us capable of really making friends or of finding true love. With the quincunx, decisions often have to be made in matters of friendship and love. At that juncture we have the opportunity of achieving a certain neutrality or detachment in our feelings—so essential if we are not to run the risk of being swept off our feet into a relationship we shall later regret. As our maturity improves in quality, love will no longer be misused as a means of satisfying desires but will become ultra-personal in the sense of being all-inclusively open and sharing. What has to be encouraged is not quantitative emotion in the form of passionate outbursts but a consistent kindliness to all living creatures.

Feelings of self-esteem (sensitiveness)

Lunar feelings of self-esteem are dependent on experience, and are responsive to the environment. As the reflecting principle, the Moon enables us to perceive and react to contacts of every kind—it represents our sensitivity. It would therefore be a mistake to think that the Moon normally gives rise to a demanding ego. The causes of faulty reactions on the emotional plane are usually to be found in an overemphatic subjectivity, where all relationships are tied up with the emotional ego. But the ego-pole ought to have such a degree of detachment that, although there is still an ego-consciousness, this consists of an optimistic awareness that, "Yes, I am sensitive and always quick to react, but I am also able to identify and understand everything which stirs my emotions."

The end result is emotional security, and a feeling of personal value, combined with independence from the environment. We are no longer relying on confirmation from others that we are worthy of friendship and love; we have been set free to decide, without being under any kind of pressure, when to socialize and when to spend some time alone.

The sooner during the ascending half-cycle we release ourselves from selfish affections, the sooner we shall acquire a healthy neutrality, equilibrium and emotional stability. Then, with a more finely tuned emotional life, we shall find ourselves more sensitive in our reactions to our surroundings. At the same time, our perception of the objective world will become increasingly differentiated and our judgment of people and events will be more balanced and accurate.

Contrasts existing in the emotional body

The greater the swings of mood between positive and nega-tive—between love and hate say—the more powerful is the pull of the ego. This egocentricity embedded in the subjective side of our feelings becomes more apparent to us with each succeeding AP aspect, especially when it is a red aspect. During such aspects we can see for ourselves how keen we are to be loved. But the main thing is to beware of falling back into bad habits. Experience must already have taught us that understanding and love should be bestowed without any thought of recompense. Love means giving and taking freely; the compulsive urge to demand affection has nothing to do with it.

That is the one extreme in red aspects to the Moon; the other is when the individual lives for others in a self-sacrificing way and completely neglects his own interests. Egoism (but here a covert egoism) can lie behind this form of behavior, too, when the self-sacrifice is made in the hope of being loved. A vain hope this, because unrestrained giving and giving way to others is seldom rewarded as it would seem to deserve. Any extremes in our emotional life will lead to disappointments and instability. Nevertheless, during such periods, we learn a great deal about ourselves and others and about our relationships to them—especially during the green aspects.

The childlike Moon ego: spontaneity

A further effect of the Age Point aspect to the Moon depends on an essential quality of a well-developed Moon ego: spontaneity. In this respect the Moon is quite different from the Sun or Saturn. The Moon always encourages spontaneous reactions, because it represents the principle of changeableness. Such reactions cannot be planned in advance, but spring out of a given situation in the here and now. Spontaneity demands that we keep on our toes so to speak; it guarantees an optimal flow of information and brings increased learning capacity.

Children, who are so governed by the Moon, exhibit this spontaneity to a high degree, especially when in the care of their mothers. As is well-known, a child reacts in a direct and lively manner, is open in approach, and only gradually becomes more constrained under the guidance of its parents. The child's natural spontaneity is the proper attribute of the Moon, and will not be entirely lost during life. In spite of all demands and the struggle for existence, we can always rekindle our spontaneity and sensitivity if we set out minds to do so. This ought to be the aim of Moon-based development and it will enable us to remain capable of loving and of being surrounded by those who love us right down to a good old age. Of course, this will be easier for us to manage under green or blue aspects than under the red ones.

● Saturn

Saturn builds the physical pole of our personality. It gives physical reality, of which the vital instinct is this: I must survive, I must function properly. The supreme law of Saturn is security, and the struggle for security takes place on all three planes of human existence. Thus it is not only the body which craves safety; the soul and spirit long for it too. Looked at from another angle, Saturn is also our memory. It helps us to retain our experiences so that we can later interpret them. We gather them for future reference. The disadvantage is the ease with which anxiety arises out of all our gathering and hoarding of memories—and out of our security-mindedness; an anxiety lest something unfortunate should happen. And so we find the need to set up some form of protection. Saturn is the opposite number of the Sun. The latter as the active, expansive principle, and Saturn as the limiting principle, often counteract one another in us. Under the influence of Saturn, we are concerned not to spread ourselves but to keep a grip on things, people, or positions.

Transit (Conjunction)

It is chiefly the desire for security that is activated at the transit of Saturn. We are increasingly inclined to hang on to our gains—and also to lost causes. Owing to our own inflexibility, life is often turned into a sort of prison from which we may find it hard to break out, especially when anxiety gets the upper hand and we fight shy of changing. Then we cordon ourselves off and deliberately put ourselves out of bounds to the world at large. Such static blocking-up is the negative side of Saturn, and no concessions should be made to it. If we do fasten the shutters, so to speak, we are as good as buried alive, and are cut off from all the productive forces of nature. We expose ourselves to a risky state of dependency. We can no longer consciously take part in life. Events trample over us because we no longer have any control over them, and they leave us pressed down even further into our rut. To seek safety in non-acceptance is the wrong reaction to a Saturn aspect. Nature herself knows no complete standstill, but is borne along by continual rhythmic fluctuation and change.

At times, Fate seems to have us on the rack and it feels as if we are about to be broken. It is then that we have to behave accommodatingly. Some of our quite justified demands may have to go. Recognition of this principle is the essential step required of us at every aspect between the Age Point and Saturn. At the transit, we can learn to assume responsibility for our lives. Saturn, as an ego planet, bestows material competence, security, and inner competence—but only when we gain the insight that so much we encounter is already within us.

The house position of Saturn

The house occupied by Saturn frequently marks the area in which the native likes to complain he is having a bad time. If it is in the seventh house (or partnership) for example, he might make allegations that as soon as his wife married him, she tied him down, imposed her will on him, and has kept him at her beck and call ever since. But, when the Age Point transits Saturn, he may realize that his inherent weakness in the area of partnership has brought him a dominating spouse, and that he was half-wanting to be ruled by her. Armed with this amount of self-knowledge, he may find it possible to insist on his rights. Meanwhile, he still grumbles. Similarly, those with Saturn in the eighth house tend to blame society, those with Saturn in the sixth house will blame an employer or colleagues, and those with the planet in the fifth house will blame circumstances for faults partly their own. The same goes for the other houses.

The AP aspects and aspect-cycle of Saturn

As already mentioned, Saturn chiefly represents the physical ego or bodily consciousness. Therefore, with the advent of any Age Point aspects we should take extra care of our physical health and safety, and should cultivate the ability to sense how we are and what is the current state of the environment. In this way we shall improve the efficiency of our lives.

Even where the five intermediate aspects are concerned, it would be a mistake to view security as static, and to shut ourselves away behind stone walls as it were. The body's true boundary is the skin. When surrounded by other boundaries (other bodies) we instinctively grasp this fact and react accordingly. Boundaries also contain barriers, but it is possible to negotiate these by an elastic and sensitive response to the demands of life. Especially is this true of the mental realm, where a closed and static picture of the world brings spiritual death. But if we can overcome the trepidation felt from Saturn's aspects and are ready to accept what is endeavoring to grow within us, we shall gain in self-assurance—a self-assurance that will enable us to accomplish difficult tasks. The ability to mount a successful challenge to fate is perhaps the best gift of Saturn, and is something to which we should aspire. Our powers are brought into play, new doors open up, and we come aware of many things which were formerly out of range.

Red aspects will enable us to tear down old partitions, and to take stock of traditional opinions and cast them aside if necessary. During blue aspects, on the other hand, our reactions are rather rigid (due to habit) and there is a fairly high risk of suffering from anxiety states. Anxiety is typical of Saturn as a planetary influence and, what is more, it will only be aggravated by a determination to cling to things outworn. Of all the aspects, the opposition has the greatest braking effect on our activity and on the urge to forge ahead. Without some such opposing force however, there would be nothing to check the onward rush powered by the Sun. If we take a ride in a car with no brakes, our first outing in it is likely to be our last. It is the green aspects that provide optimum conditions for achieving an economy of forces.

Another fundamental function of Saturn is to promote economy in our expenditure of energy. We must learn how to employ our resources and to bring our energies into play as efficiently as possible—and when we speak of energies and resources we mean those that are mental and spiritual as well as those that are material. Whoever spends more than he earns, is behaving in a very un-Saturnian manner; he has no control over his means of subsistence.

The individual who has found it impossible to manage his energies can learn to do so during the Age-Point aspects. When we come up against limitations in the external world, such as impending insolvency, loss of face, illness, lack of encouragement, etc., we encounter that malefic quality attributed to Saturn in the literature. From this point of view, it is the "Dweller of the Threshold," which comes to exact payment and turn back the presumptive adept who attempts things beyond his ability. But when we learn to channel our energies effectively, Saturn brings us inner security, spontaneous confidence and a real joy in living. Younger patrons of astrology tend to see Saturn as a helpful influence which they welcome rather than dread.

• Mercury, Venus, Mars, Jupiter

When compared to the three planets of Personality, the Age Point aspects to the four planets Mercury, Venus, Mars and Jupiter appear somewhat less notable. Nevertheless, these planets do represent organs and functions in the native that are significant for his development. As already mentioned, we become more aware of the qualities of a planet when it is being transited. It is best, therefore, to cultivate an expectant attitude in order to be able to respond positively to the planetary principle and to grow in maturity. With a readiness to learn we shall develop true to pattern. Age Point aspects bring illnesses and material setbacks only when the opportunity for further development is deliberately ignored or rejected. To this extent we have a choice as to how the aspects will operate. We shall now discuss the most important effects of the AP transit (conjunction) and of the AP cycle in regard to the development of the individual planetary abilities. The intensity—positive or negative— of a planet's contact with the Age Point largely depends on the native's inner adjustment. There is no point in trying to make hard-and-fast predictions, since so much that happens to a person is determined by his character and by his conscious attitude.

• Mercury

During the AP transit, we are both eager and able to learn those things implied by Mercury's position in sign and house. Thanks to our mental nimbleness and curiousity, we are ready to explore new areas of knowledge and can glean a mass of interesting facts in the process. We may, for the first time, find that we have a good working knowledge of some subject; also that we can improve this knowledge considerably by conscious effort. The transit of Mercury improves our intellectual efficiency; professional and other successes are in the cards as we become more perceptive. The work of those of us who are still at school shows a marked improvement and lost time is made up with relative ease. For the rest, we may discover that people who once ignored us suddenly give us a hearing and take us seriously. The time is ripe for a change of job: we are ready for the new because the old has lost its fascination. In the past, perhaps, we were rather reserved, but now there are stimulating new people to meet with whom we can exchange ideas. Finally, we shall probably want to pass on our knowledge and may look for some calling in which it will be possible to do so.

During the aspect cycle a development takes place in our intellectual prowess. Mercury's medium is speech, and it gives the ability to clothe thoughts in well-chosen words that carry conviction. It also imparts a gift for languages. Its strength lies in the collecting, arranging and cataloging of ideas. Business sense, too, is displayed under its influence. Every aspect, as it arrives, will stimulate us to cultivate Mercurial characteristics, which is all to the good as long as we do not spread our interests so thin that we no longer have the energy to pursue our true path.

The negative effects are: talkativeness, sensationalism, false compromises, indecision, trying to bring everyone down to the same level, and trimming one's sails to every wind.

● Venus

When the AP transits Venus, we are more convivial and more prepared to indulge ourselves. We want to enjoy the good things in life and to avoid harsh realities. We may even fall over backwards to compromise with people. Where, in the past, we would have stuck to our guns come what may, we now seek to reach agreement. Enemies are won over and harmony replaces unrest.

Venus represents selectivity in human relationships. At the transit of the planet, we are usually acutely aware of who or what is congenial to us and the reverse. We become choosy about our friends and may want to have folks around us with whom we feel comfortable. Many of us will find that our former boon companions no longer appeal to us. In addition, Venus is the planet of the female libido. Age permitting, the transit of Venus can give a man an intense experience of the female sex. And, where a woman is concerned, she can become much more passionate and sexually demanding towards her partner. She could also get on better with other women.

As far as the AP aspect cycle is concerned, the chief point of interest is the development of our interaction with others (from mere politeness to genuine friendship) and of that esthetic sense which serves to smooth our rough edges. Venus embodies harmony and beauty, and each time she is aspected we have an opportunity to find pleasure—either in our loved ones or in material or spiritual things.

Venus takes part in all processes of selection and assimilation. At each AP aspect we are once more faced with the necessity of choosing between this and that, and will gradually improve our understanding of what our nature really requires. Many of us will have to learn when to say yes and when to say no. Others will be able to free themselves from feelings of guilt arising from faulty teaching which had hindered them from essaying anything good. Yet there is a distinct possibility (depending on the radical aspects) that we shall have to accept suffering. Venus seeks balance in all things and, where the equilibrium has been disturbed, she comes along with a counterweight to restore it. If we have been too absorbed in our little luxuries and personal comforts, the transit of Venus can make us aware of how soft and spineless we have become; we may even fall ill. And if, to avoid our responsibilities, we have abandoned independent thought in order to serve some idea, or are allowing ourselves to be ruled by a stronger personality, we shall have to face the challenge to take our destiny in our own hands again.

If on the other hand we have been self-reliant in the past, and have avoided close relationships, we shall become more approachable during the Venusian aspect. We shall start looking for friendship and love—and are quite likely to find the right partner.

The negative aspects are: indulgence, opportunism, presumption, lack of reliability, flightiness, excessive sexual demands in the female, poor sexual performance or effeminacy in the man.

● Mars

When the AP transits Mars our performance is improved. We perceive a new strength enabling us to do things which have needed tackling for a long time. Suddenly we have the courage to do what has to be done; our nervousness is gone. Those of us who are normally low on motivation gain an exhilarating sense of freedom. We venture into the unknown and set to work to gain our ends. At the same time, we are usually rather impatient and want to put our plans into immediate effect. Mars is the male libido planet and frequently brings women liaisons with the opposite sex. In men it helps to activate their potency and sense of machismo and so leads to more intense love-making. The transit is a positive period for our hopes and wishes.

Before making any rash moves, however, we should study the aspects in the radix. Perhaps we are overestimating our strengths, or flattering ourselves too much on our chances. After all, our resources may be great but they are not unlimited. Unless sign and house position decree otherwise, we are inclined to take an exaggerated view of things; our defense mechanisms and our pugnacity are increased, too, and should be checked for motivation.

During the AP cycle there is a development of our motor energy and such a blind willingness to get on with things that we are liable to go storming forward regardless of risk. During this cycle, therefore, we shall have ample opportunity to discover what we are really capable of doing—usually through crises arising at the various aspects. We learn from Mars by passing through the fire, by living experience, and not by mere observation or book knowledge. No doubt we shall burn our fingers more than once before we acquire wisdom. The goal of development during the martian cycle is to gain awareness of our motoric driving power. How long this will take depends on the planets associated with Mars. Alternatively, we can consciously employ the energy and executive power of the red planet to set things in motion again after a time of repose or relaxation.

The negative effects are: injudicious dealings, violence, a love of aggression and destruction, excessive carnal desire and male chauvinism, conflicts and schisms.

● Jupiter

Our powers of perception and observation are improved and we see the world and our own possibilities in a truer light. We have a clear appreciation of what is true and what false in ourselves and others. Jupiter represents the sum-total of all the senses; at conjunction it is stimulated and wide-awake. Discernment, a sense of values and an appreciation of quality are distinctly activated. Perhaps we shall be horrified by the knowledge of the mistakes we have already made. Things are often seen in their right proportions for the first time and our system of values may benefit by growing in scope. For Jupiter does indeed bring an extension of consciousness and allows the wider connections between things to be seen. The result is great assurance, spiritual growth, and a knowledge of inner motivations: all of which frees us of any doubts we may have had about our eventual success. We are now conscious of our best qualities and can turn them to good account. It was not for nothing that traditional astrology called Jupiter the "Greater Fortune."

During the AP cycle of Jupiter there is a development of our sense perceptions. In the ascending half-cycle the latter are sharpened; our powers of observation become better and more precise and we have a truer understanding of the realities of life. It is easier for us to recognize deceptions, illusions and untruths; we react to wrong attitudes in ourselves and others with greater awareness and do not labor under so many false impressions. What we do is more worthy of us, and we become wiser, more tolerant and more impartial. The clearer our perceptions, the more accurately we shall judge matters and, as the years go by we shall gain a clearer insight into the hidden "machinery" that rules appearances. This will give us more freedom in the way we express ourselves. The end of the cycle is often a time when everything fits perfectly into place, even those things which once bothered us or filled us with dread. For one of the functions of Jupiter is to release our self-healing powers.

The negative effects are: delusions and pride, an attitude of "I know best," boasting, arrogance, insubordination, light-mindedness, irresponsibility.

• Uranus, Neptune, Pluto

With the three more recently discovered planets we come to respresentatives of mental or spiritual faculties which are for the most part latent within us. During the AP cycle these can be developed. In figure 1.3.4 on page 55, we see these "newer" planets placed by themselves above the three main planets. This is because we regard them as "higher ego principles" or as organs of the so-called "higher self"—Uranus as the creative intelligence, Neptune as the higher love principle, and Pluto as spiritual will-power. In their purest form they are active only in a person who has largely succeeded in integrating his threefold personality and is unselfishly trying to help forward the evolution of the race. However, for the most part they operate as a collective fate, by which those who ignore the wider issues are often developed more harshly, and in spite of themselves.

During the AP aspect cycles of the three newer planets, we have opportunity for a gradual increase in our understanding of the true nature of these fundamental spiritual principles. They belong to transpersonal (suprapersonal) regions in which everything has to take place without the intervention of the ego; that is to say, without conscious purpose or self-assertion. If we are not calm and collected we shall not be able to handle them properly, and this is the reason why they so often exercise a disruptive effect, especially on selfish plans.

All AP aspects to the three spiritual planets, but especially the conjunction, perform transmutations on the elements that control our behavior. They mobilize forces within us that are inspirational and consciousness-expanding; forces that have a cleansing action but are often disrupting, too. It may well happen that, when the AP transits one of them, we begin to take an interest in spiritual topics and activities; or circumstances may take a hand in introducing us to transcendental dimensions.

● **Uranus**

Often, when the Age Point transits Uranus, we are visited by a spirit of unrest and have the feeling that something completely new is about to happen. We begin to wonder if the way we are living is as it should be. The very possibility that it may not be so can make us anxious and disturbed and open a door to new vistas, fresh concepts. We have a desire to investigate, and our creative intelligence is stimulated. There is a wish to know what lies beyond our everyday world. Therefore, at the time of transit, we are likely to come across some arcane volumes or some people who will introduce us to new thought structures (*e.g.*, to astrology). Such finds or encounters often impart a shock which upsets the values on which we have so far relied. Our old world sinks below the waves of life and a new world rises to view.

An important Uranian motive is to gain security through knowledge—not the narrow, personal security of Saturn, but a more spiritual and spacious type of security. The native wants to penetrate deeper into the secrets of life and to learn the laws of human, of planetary, and even of cosmic development. His attitudes undergo a transformation and a "Saul" may be converted into a "Paul." The life-style is altered and, maybe the traditional way of doing things is rejected out-of-hand in typical Uranian style. In a word, he experiences a revolutionary change of consciousness.

During the AP aspect-cycle we gradually become acclimatized to fresh, conscious attitudes. As aspects come along, we experience an urge of varying intensity to leave behind the frontiers of the known, to expand our consciousness, and to improve the running of our lives and our sense of security by an input of new knowledge. In the aspects succeeding the conjunction, we are still feeling our way and are ready to fall back on the tried and trusted at a moment's notice. The start of the spiritual path is beset by doubts, which are dispelled only a few at a time. Upon our first entry into spiritual dimensions, we are still unsure whether or not we are moving in the right direction. We take pains to make things secure for ourselves and, especially at the quincunx, tend to be tormented by spasms of doubt. These, however, serve to develop our awareness and our autonomy of thought. But by opposition at the latest we should have obtained clear indications of the reality of spiritual, impalpable things. As time goes by, we become more successful at integrating the effects of Uranus with our creative intelligence. This puts us in possession of a bubbling spring of inspiration: a source of originality and inner strength.

The negative effects are: willfulness and defiant behavior, nervous impatience, eccentricities, revolutionary notions, indiscriminate attacks on the establishment (terrorism), equating levelling with progress, technophilia, loss of compassion, know-it-all arrogance.

● Neptune

At AP transit over Neptune, our sensibilities are stimulated. We find ourselves able to participate in forms of communication in the external world of which we were hitherto unaware, even though they were always present. Therefore, such transits frequently cause indescribable feelings; we are uncannily open to the world around us, eavesdropping dreamily on our own thought processes and picking up the faintest signals coming from our immediate environment. Nepture wires us into the communications network linking every human being. Something like the mysterious ether, it is invisible to the eye, yet can be detected by a higher sense than sight. Often we experience through its agency the unity of all living creatures and, when Neptune is transited, our identification mechanism is put into operation. We can become so familiar with matters normally beyond our scope that we identify with them. And when, as may happen at such times, we lose ourselves in unrestrained love for another person, we step at that moment beyond the bounds of the ego.

From a different point of view, Neptune embodies the principle of ideal love: the highest we can conceive, and one for which we yearn our life long. This is a living force, which thrusts us past every barrier separating man from man and affords us a glimpse of the Other's inmost self. The Neptunian principle of universal love continues to unfold in us during the AP aspect-cycle, and it is by means of this that we come to understand—through empathy—the immeasurable universe, and to incorporate it in us in a certain sense. Once we begin to appreciate the extent of the unity underlying all things, we shall develop social and altruistic motives; which may well display some touches of extremism on occasion if we have previously been unduly self-seeking and materialistic. When we consciously unlock the true meaning of Neptune, every aspect made by the Age Point will bring a change in motivation, and often, in turn, a change of mind. With each aspect, our ideals, our humanity, and our social conscience are put to the test. In the ascending part of the aspect cycle, we can add further growth to our Neptunian qualities and, in the descending part, may be able to do much good to the underprivileged, to the disabled and in short to all who suffer.

Neptune, as the principle of all-inclusiveness, the transcender of limitations, has the power to evoke many strange and disconcerting emotions during the intermediate stages. As a primordial spiritual principle (along with the two other spiritual planets), it can provide the inner experiences we need to recognize the existence of something beyond the purely material. But it has to be remembered that, on leaving behind the substantial, we can go astray (if the aspects incite us) in realms of phantasy, in dreams or in the dark world of the unconsicous, and finally sink in a bottomless morass. In extreme cases we may fall at this time into the hands of deceivers who, disguising their bad intentions under a cloak of love or kindness and taking advantage of our susceptibility, will use us for their own ends, inducing us to make many sacrifices—even material sacrifices—on their behalf. Because we seem to lose our natural protection when exposed to the influence of Nepture, we come under the sway of trends of all sorts according to the aspects. This is why Neptune has a rather unsavory reputation in classical astrology. Numerous perversions and diseases, delusions and deceptions, are ascribed to it. Entering its influence is said to be like entering a poisonous fog; yet a clear light breaks once we have learned its lesson of identification with the highest love ideal, with Christ, with universal charity.

The negative effects are: deception, temptation, addiction to drugs of any kind, exaggerated sensitivity (hysteria), debilitated will, nebulous intellect, hallucination, anxiety, unreliability, fraud.

● Pluto

Pluto represents our prototype, our pneuma. Spiritually, it is the image of the higher man or overman to which we ought to be conformed. At the time of AP transit, we become capable and willing to make a change in ourselves. As the form-changing principle, it is initiating the tremendous metamorphoses going on in our times and in individual consciousness too. The hand of Pluto will often tear off any mask which is not representative of our true ego. Pluto is the harbinger of a higher stage of development and announces to our astonished ears that the world is different from what we thought it was; it pulls aside the surface of things to show us their inner workings. How significant it is, then, that the time of its discovery in 1930 also saw the splitting of the atom!

During the AP transit of Pluto it is not unusual for the native to be confronted with his "shadow." His compulsions and inadequacies become painfully obvious. Matters which have been put to one side half-finished now clamor for attention; repressions grow hard to live with. Perhaps the conscience wakes up and persuades the native to try and turn over a new leaf. Probably he will be able to see himself "warts and all" and will know what he has to do to improve. One thing at least is clear: old forms have to be abandoned and old rules scrapped; risks must be faced and anxieties overcome. In individual development, one frequently senses an influx of fresh energy, because Pluto activates the nuclear forces involved in one's deepest motivation. It impinges directly on the center of a person's being and releases the energies of the will; which then tend to bring him in line with his penuma—or image of his higher self. Far-reaching changes take place in the ego, changes spilling over into everyday life which may even alter the appearance. It is impossible to continue in the same old rut.

During the AP aspect-cycle, the degree to which we possess the experience and maturity required to cooperate with our higher self will depend on the quadrant in which we encounter this formidable Pluto-factor in our lives. A refined sense of purpose is the pre-requisite for overcoming the problems posed at every Age Point aspect. A contemplative approach to the alterations in the guiding imagery will often promote inner harmony. At each aspect we catch a partial glimpse of the sort of persons we ought to be, and of how we ought to be motivated in order to fulfill our task in life and grow to our true spiritual stature. Visions seen during Plutonian aspects should always be taken seriously, not treated as foolish fancies; even when we wonder whether we, with our modest talents, are capable of fulfilling them.

As the representative of our personal nuclear energy, Pluto is always endeavoring to bring us to perfection as soon as possible. Although perfection in this context is a relative term, each aspect to the planet does in fact bring us further forward along the road to it. At one time our characters need to have something trimmed off, and at others they need to have something added. Though the process can be painful, it is necessary to accept whatever Pluto brings. Our small wills have to be blended with the greater Will. With the advent of each aspect, we are confronted by opportunities we have not yet taken, opportunities we are not certain how to handle perhaps; but however much plagued by anxiety we may be, there is no further chance to shirk or pull back—Pluto's power is absolute. Pluto has to do with death and rebirth, with the transformation of one form of consciousness into another.

In all aspects of Pluto we are usually "on our own" and have to use our unaided will-power to achieve the goals we have glimpsed.

When we think there is nothing more we can do, that our affairs are out of control and that we might as well give up, it is then that the will-power of Pluto takes over the reins. And all activities which serve others, not self, have a positive outcome.

The negative effects are: manipulation of friends and associates, aggression in the name of higher authority, sexual magic, delusions of grandeur ("guru-trips"), destructive urges, premonitions of disaster, susceptibility to mass hysteria, death wishes.

● The Nodes of the Moon

The Nodes of the Moon are not planets, that is to say, they are not primary principles incorporated in bodies in space and radiating their influence to us, but they are in fact the points where the (apparent) orbit of the Sun and the orbit of the Moon cross each other. The point where the Moon appears to cross the Sun's orbit from south to north when travelling in its own path is called the ascending node (or Dragon's head), and the point where it crosses from north to south is called the descending node (or Dragon's Tail). We confine ourselves to marking the ascending node in horoscopes because, according to its placement in house (though not in sign), this node indicates the way of our spiritual ascent. It is particularly significant from the point of view of the Age Point, since that has so much to tell us about our development.

The AP transit often signposts the exit from blind alleys. Now it is the function of the ascending node to show the way forward, whereas the descending node (on the diametrically opposite side of the chart) shows the way back. Although the latter is usually more accessible, a fully aware person chooses the former. At the AP transit of the ascending node we have an understanding of what will aid our progress. We get into situations helpful to our spiritual destiny and meet people who can put us on the right track. It is not unusual, in fact, to find students of psychological astrology taking up their studies when the AP makes contact with one of the nodes in their charts.

With every aspect to the Dragon's Head, there is a notable opportunity for further development. At the same time, we discover what we must do to accelerate or round off our current development. In this connection we may need to gain a better understanding of the radical house position of the node. This indicates the area in which the significant activity will take place, the area in which there are lessons to be learned.

The above-mentioned opportunity for further development offered at each AP aspect can come to us either in the form of a fresh capacity for inner effort, or in the form of favorable external circumstances. Often we have a little idea of what is good for our development, but when the Moon's node is reached, our values may make a U-turn and things which were materially beneficial are seen to be damaging to our spiritual growth.

The negative effects are: avoidance of genuine effort, or a disposition to take the easy way out and to plod along in the same old rut in a self-satisfied mood.

Chapter 5

Age Progression in Professional Counseling

Introduction—The significance of the Lunar Node—The three personality planets: Sun, Moon, and Saturn—Age Progression and accurate timing—The impressions of early childhood—An example from consulting work—Five examples from our case books

● Introduction

Use of the Age Point is a great help in counselling. It provides us with an immediate understanding of the inner workings of questions involving education, employment and partnership, and of what lies behind life crises or turning points in spiritual growth. In psychological counselling the birth chart is already being used as a diagnostic instrument by many professional advisers; but now we have Age Progression as an outstanding additional analytical tool of incalculable worth for progressing a chart. It shows us, in an unequivocal manner, the exact mental and spiritual situation of an individual at a given point in time, together with a general survey of the whole course of his or her life with all its problems and potential for development.

Serious astrologers and psychologists often try to work with the classical methods of direction; but it is time-consuming to sort out the meaning of all the traditional transits and directions for a particular moment (that of consultation say). And yet that is what has to be done when these methods are employed, if the client's current situation is to be correctly assessed. Some consultants try to simplify matters by confining themselves to only one of the classical methods of direction, and by so doing fail to make a well-rounded judgment of the current situation of the person seeking their help. What they have to tell is necessarily sketchy, and it is all too easy for them to project their own thoughts and wishes onto the client for want of properly researched material.

Here the Age Progression system offers itself as a genuine alternative which, when properly understood, yields by the simplest means both the basic theme and the detailed structural patterns of the client's total character as it exists at a given moment in time. It is a tremendous asset to the counsellor to be able to identify the counsellee's situation from a glance at his or her radical chart. The psychotherapist, by tracing the course of the Age Point, can immediately spot acute problems and the duration of chronic depressions, etc., and can adjust his treatments accordingly. He can discuss with the client the influences and possibilities he has seen in the chart, and has the advantage of knowing when a depressive phase will end and when a "better" period will begin. Not only is time saved by this procedure, but it is possible to study the personality of the individual very intensively and to bring about the release of his constructive forces. Much more time would be required to achieve comparable results by the usual psychological techniques.

Once the trained counsellor or therapist knows how to read a client's chart correctly, he will now straight away why the latter has come to consult him. He will see the psychological reason for the given problem, since the Age Point reveals the current state of development in the horoscope. Also revealed are the main and side issues involved, the tasks which ought to be taken in hand, and the hindrances to be overcome. Advice can be given on the immediately available and quickest solutions.

It is important for counsellor and client to work together. A good therapist will go through the horoscope and the movement of the Age Point with the patient. The effect will be much more profound and there will be considerably less danger of transference on the part of the client. The horoscope is a neutral means of diagnosis, and its very neutrality greatly reduces the risk of transference. What is more, since it is not the counsellor with his or her personal opinions of the client, but the horoscope, measuring the problem against the constellations, that provides the key to the situation, the subjective approach is ruled out.

In any case, what is wanted in astrological counselling is not lengthy chart analyses so much as the cultivation of a genuine approach to the other person in order to begin the consultation on common ground. Then the client will not feel that he or she is being manipulated, but will become less nervous and will be able to relax in an atmosphere of frankness and mutual trust.

In the first place, our aim is to help the other person. This has to be the main motive in every attempt to give advice. To be successful, the counsellor must be a good listener, because people instantly detect whether someone is really interested in them or not. What is required is the wish to be sincere and the rejection of any impulse to model others according to some preconceived pattern.

A genuinely helpful approach is often crucial for the inner experience of the person being counselled: the horizon may be expanded and the viewpoint changed. With the help of the birth chart, the counsellor can make the client conscious of his or her deepest motivations and goals, can make them feel properly understood and recognized. Nevertheless, the horoscope is neutral: it remains an objective witness to the life situation of the individual. It does not take the place of the adviser, who can be selective in what he says, but is more in the nature of a "tide table" giving the ebb and flow of the psyche; as such, it enables the individual to view his problems more objectively and to set sail on fresh ventures.

● The Significance of the Node

Frequently we find people coming for advice just as their Age Point is transiting the Moon's ascending node. From an astrological psychological point of view, this is interpreted as the first step in further development. It is the starting point, the place of least resistance, which has to be activated and brought into consciousness because it is directly involved in mental or physical difficulties. People usually have some inkling of where this starting point lies, but need to have it positively identified for them before they can take action. The house containing the lunar node indicates the area in which current problems have to be broached, and the adviser must consider first the Age Point and then the node, if any real help is to be given.

● The Three Personality Planets:
Sun, Moon, Saturn

The three personality planets (Sun, Moon and Saturn) are important, too, in astrological counselling, and represent the three poles of the ego. The Sun is the ego of the mental plane, the thought ego; the Moon is the emotional ego; Saturn is the physical ego or body consciousness. Many mental disturbances are due to the fact that one of these three poles is being over-stimulated and the body is not functioning as a unit. It is true, of course, that each of the three ego-poles has a characteristic time of development in a person's life: normally, the physical body develops in the first third of life, the emotions develop in the second third, and the understanding develops in the final third. In individual cases, however, one or another factor comes into prominence according to the positions of the three main planets in the horoscope, and so, during certain periods of the native's life (and sometimes throughout his or her life) the harmony between them is lacking. Thus hopes and wishes may not be in keeping with mental aims or with physical capacities. On occasion, the physical strength is stretched too far by the conflict between the various spheres of the ego, and the result is psychosomatic illness.

When the person who comes for a consultation happens to have the Age Point transiting one of the three main planets in his or her chart, the problem is always to be found in the area of personal development and, depending on the planet involved, this problem has to do with material (Saturn), emotional (Moon), or mental (Sun) uncertainties and preoccupations affecting the ego. It is of the utmost importance that these factors be integrated within the characted as a whole. If there is a weakness somewhere in the ego— and, if so, the horoscope will show it—mental disorders such as depression or hysteria are possible, often because the native has not experienced success on any of the three planes.

In judging the Age Point aspects to the main planets, it is necessary to ask whether we are concerned with the development of the personality in the outside world, or are concerned with the growth of the spiritual man internally. Much depends on the age and mental development of the individual, of course, but, provided we know the answer to the above question when interpreting the aspects, we should be able to improve our understanding of our own situation and that of others.

Self-confidence is more or less marked according to the radical aspects and house positions of these three planets, even though, to begin with, we seldom possess as much self-confidence as we should like. The unfolding of our tripartite personality is an on-going process which is never complete. It is generally accepted that the key factor in the process is external success, or feedback from the environment. Often this is the only factor considered; the assumption being that the more recognition there is from the outside world, the stronger the self-confidence will be. Success is most important for creating a stable personality; because the individual feels more sure of himself, he feels that he knows how to handle himself in order to get the best out of any situation.

But, as already mentioned, in Age Progression we are concerned not simply with increasing self-confidence but also with the development of the "inner person" of those whose motives and actions are guided by a spirit of true humanity. The emphasis here is on the ethical side of astrology about which we do not know very much, although increasing attention is being paid to it in modern times. In the AP aspects to the three personality planets there is therefore always an opportunity for spiritual development, provided we gain a deeper insight into ourselves, our inner goals, and our spiritual guidelines. In the process of reaching a higher degree of self-awareness, the individual changes continuously: at each stage of life, in each house, at each Low Point in the signs, and with every increase in consciousness.

In brief, what we are looking at is the change from an egocentric individual to a consciously responsible, free individual who recognizes the Self as part of the Whole and is able to care for others. The integrated personality is freed from obsession with its own interests in order to concentrate on higher tasks benefiting the community. From a spiritual point of view, the individual outgrows himself or herself by making a creative contribution to evolution. Therefore we should take seriously in this sense all AP aspects to the main planets and should try to extract as much good as possible from the development of the personality and from the individuation process. It is extremely important to delineate with care the threefold structure of the personality in the radix, recognizing any weaknesses in the ego and any problems to do with parents or with superiority or inferiority complexes. The meanings of AP aspects to the three personality planets were discussed in the previous chapter.

• Age Progression and Accurate Timing

In considering the psychological application of the Age Point, it cannot be sufficiently stressed that the Age Point mainly indicates mental and spiritual development processes, which are usually initiated by internal and only seldom by external events. A further salient point is that these processes tend to be set in motion before the exact time of AP conjunction with a planet, sensitive point or cusp.

Frequently it is hard to tell when a certain period of development commenced; although many a time the first planetary contact or aspect has a causative effect, as we shall see later in the section on "impressions in early childhood." It is important to know that some events will not occur until certain changes have taken place in our behavior, our attitude to life or our mental attunement. From a psychological point of view, the exact date of an event is unimportant, as each new stage in life represents a process that has a beginning, a climax and an end, and lasts for a fixed time. Since this is a rather revolutionary concept, we shall illustrate it by means of an example (see figure 1.5.1.)

In our example, at the age of thirty-one, the Age Point transits a natal Sun posited just beyond the sixth cusp in the radix, and the

Figure 1.5.1. An Age Point transit to the radical Sun causes a confirmation of consciousness.

native may find that, during the preceding year, he has had to face the problem of self-determination with regard to his inner vocation, being much preoccupied, both before and after the transit, with what headway he can make in his job or profession. Moreover, in our example, the Sun has a great deal to do with self-confidence. Perhaps the acquisition of some special skill has given self-confidence a boost. Or perhaps the native's self-respect has been injured by slights or rebuffs when he has not been able to come up to the mark. In such instances, the connection between inner cause and outer effect is clearly exhibited.

Death of the father

Another example might be the death of the father. This traumatic event, with all its material and familial results, is likely to be indicated by Age-Point aspects in the charts both of the deceased and of the bereaved. The bereaved person will find it difficult to assimilate the event in a way helpful to his own development and maturity if he tries to dispose of it as quickly and as painlessly as possible. He should be thinking not simply that the father's "time had come," but that he himself is very much involved in this, the last step in the long and often heavy process of separation from his father. What was not achieved at the age of sixteen or twenty, in spite of all kicking over the traces, and later failed to occur "according to plan" owing to repression, is suddenly forced on the native by an external occurrence. If he can manage to see the death not simply as something distressing that has happened "out there," but as a challenge to further self-development, the sad event will be filled with more meaning than can be found in the elaborate ritual of a funeral.

Of course, such events do not keep on happening from one minute to the next but take time to be experienced. They build up slowly, reach their peak and then subside. The corresponding inner processes also continue over a period of months—as may be seen from the locus of the Age Point. Each aspect sits, so to speak, atop an intensity curve and, at the point in time indicated by the high point on the curve, an event of considerable importance can occur. Nevertheless, the Age Point starts to make its influence felt long before this. At the beginning of the slow rise, a flanking event may anticipate the main theme and bring interesting side-effects. Together with what is yet to come in the descending portion of the curve, the whole makes up an experience which is "greater than the sum of its parts."

Conclusion

To be able to use the Age Point Progression system, we do not need to know the exact timing of an event, but simply the year, the time of year or (at most) the month. We do not require to know the exact day because, as already explained, we are dealing with processes of development that extend over periods longer than a day. Usually, it would be impossible for us to tell just when there began to stir within us some feeling of unrest, some new idea, which perhaps took hold of our whole personality and radically altered our attitude to life and to other people. In handling Age Point Progression, we must learn to think in terms of a movement through time, of cycles and changes, instead of in terms of given moments as shown in figure 1.5.2.

Adopting the latter mode of thought was an error perpetrated by classical astrology, which was so preoccupied with pinpointing exact times that the very credit of the art came to depend on the ability to make accurate predictions. Being put to the proof in such an extreme fashion has done great damage to astrology, especially as many of the predictions failed to come true on time, and it cannot be repeated too often that we, with the advantage of today's psychological knowledge, ought to turn away from event-orientated thinking in order to concentrate on development-orientated thinking.

Figure 1.5.2. The intensity of pre- and post-effects of the Age Point.

● Impressions in Early Childhood

In recent decades, psychological researchers have discovered that experiences, especially those of childhood, will continue to exert a compelling pressure on our thoughts, emotions and behavior so long as they lie hidden in the unconscious. As soon as their memories are made conscious, their power is broken and we can set about counteracting their effects. Even our inherited or acquired characteristics govern us only until, however slowly, we manage to extirpate wrong attitudes. Naturally, the processes of self-recognition do not remove our innate or imparted flaws all at once, but they do enable us to distance ourselves from them and to adopt a new point of view. We are no longer sold into a helpless slavery to unconscious forces, but are in possession of the knowledge that could set us free.

It is here that Age Progression can assist us. All transits and oppositions affecting planets in the first quadrant (*i.e.*, affecting the first eighteen years of life) unequivocally point to such childhood impressions. In self-analysis and in therapy, it is essential to institute a thorough investigation of the events indicated, however small and insignificant they may seem to be. It is astounding to discover the close connection they have with later behavior patterns, patterns which can be gradually altered only through the release into consciousness and the mature understanding of these self-same events.

Age 0-18

The period when the environment makes the strongest impact on the character is from 0-18 years. In the natal chart this is represented by the first quadrant, running from the AC to the IC. Note that the whole quadrant is involved here, and that the environmental influence remains strong right up to the threshold of independence.

As a rule, planets posited in the first quadrant make a more powerful impression on the youngster and adolescent than do those distributed in other parts of the chart. In psychology, we speak of traumatic events: but by traumas we do not intend simply the unpleasant, negative occurrences; the positive ones are included, too. They are traumatic for the reason that our conscious mind refuses to have anything to do with them. Frequently they generate complexes and behavioral reflexes later in life without our being able to figure where the connection lies. Prolonged self-observation may be required before the link is found; unless, of course, we call in the services of Age Progression. Then it becomes relatively easy to see, from the planetary positions in the first quadrant, the operation of cause and effect, and thus to start making a change.

Even severe psychological complexes can be rooted in childhood's impressionable years. Almost any planet standing in the first quadrant points to a childhood trauma, positive or negative. However, a distinction has to be made between strong and weak effects. The planets are at their most powerful in this regard when in houses one and two, representing the ages from birth to twelve years old. This period of childhood finds the young person completely dependent on his environment because he is unable to look after himself. Since his will is still relatively weak and his ego undeveloped, his mother or surrogate mother is free to stamp her personality on him and to mould him in her chosen image. Yet, by the same token, she (like other factors in his environment) may be a source of traumas.

The presence of planets in the first and second houses in hard aspect to some other planet or planets, will suggest that the native was probably much under the influence of his environment at a certain period. If he was, then they will reveal the time of the formative experiences.

When there are no planets in the first quadrant, the question arises: "Were there not, during childhood, any impressions strong enough to give rise to traumas or complexes?" For the answer, we

Figure 1.5.3. Secondary aspects involved in Age Progression.

have to take a look at the opposite section of the chart. It is practically certain that in the third quadrant there will be planets to oppose the Age Point while it is tracking the native's childhood phase. These have a formative effect almost as strong as that of planets transited by the Age Point in the first three houses. In other words, the third-quadrant opposition like the first-quadrant conjunction usually indicates events which have had a formative influence on character during the first eighteen years of life— influences which are responsible for certain behavior patterns later on.

The other aspects (for example, the square, trine, sextile and quincunx) are of secondary importance in this respect; though to some extent they prepare the way for, or perhaps weaken, the main effect according to the direction from which they are cast.

Figure 1.5.3 shows a planet situated at 20° Aquarius in the second house. The first house is empty; but 20° Capricorn in the first house is in 30° aspect to the planet in the second house. This point represents a preliminary impression as far as the planet at 20° Aquarius in the second house is concerned. Suppose, now, that the Age Point transits a planet (Saturn in our example) at 20° Aquarius; it is likely that at the age of nine years the primary impression will be experienced as an essentially psychological event. In addition, however, at the age of four (represented by 20° Capricorn) a secondary impression has already made itself felt. The child has been sensitized in advance by a somewhat similar experience, though not with such trauma as he will undergo at the age of nine.

Similar considerations apply if a planet is placed at 20° Leo in the same chart. The transit of 20° Capricorn in the first house makes a 150 degree angle (or quincunx) to this planet. Here, too, we are looking at a preliminary impression. The opposition at 20° Aquarius gives the time of the major influence. All other aspects from the following signs represent subsequent impressions which may help to resolve any problem that has arisen.

The square activates the problem. To stay with our example, an emotional experience can occur when the Age Point makes a square to 20° Aquarius from 20° Taurus. The problem refuses to be ignored any longer. Squares can have a shattering yet clarifying effect, but do not necessarily enable us to come to terms with our difficulties. Further information on this point will be found in the chapter on "Age Point Aspects."

Figure 1.5.4. We need one half an Age Point (or 36 years) to overcome early impressions.

Generally speaking, the following points should be observed when judging the relationship of the aspects to early impressions:

1. The impression itself is made, not at the square but at the conjunction or opposition;

2. The solution of the problem does not appear until the AP has moved 180° on from the point marking where the problem arises.

3. In the intermediate aspects, the nuances of the situation become increasingly apparent and the problem starts to come within range of the conscious mind ready for eventual solution at the age represented by the opposition.

In our example, the actual solution of the problem indicated in the second house will not be possible until the age shown by the transit of the Age Point through the eighth house; that is to say at some age between forty-two and forty-eight or ca. forty-four years. (See figure 1.5.4.) Psychologically speaking it is interesting to note that usually we need thirty-six years (or half the full AP cycle) to extricate ourselves from the consequences of early impressions or to overcome a faulty reaction.

• An Example from Consulting Work

It is quite surprising what one finds when working through the chart positions for the first eighteen years of a client's life. "What experience did you have when you were seven years old?" we might ask, on noting the Age Point transit of the Sun (square Saturn) in the second house.

Figure 1.5.5 illustrates a case of this kind. The lady who consulted us did not take long in identifying her problem and soon volunteered the information that her parents were divorced when she was seven years old. As a result she was parted from her mother, because her father was awarded custody of her and of her brothers and sisters. The separation caused her a great deal of suffering; all the more so as she could not understand what was going on. Psychological-cum-astrological interviews elicited that she had secretly believed that it was on her account that her mother had gone away. Later in life, inexplicable guilt feelings would rise from her unconscious to stand in the way of any close relationship and to torment her with the dread that the loved one would desert her. This fear of loss went hand in hand with a fear of destitution, which became very acute at the age of twenty-nine when the Age Point was conjunct the Sun and square to Saturn. At that age she married and became the breadwinner of the family to enable her husband to continue his studies. It was not until the opposition was reached, when she was forty-nine years old, that her husband succeeded in his profession and she was set free from financial worries.

What really happened here was a development process undergone by her own personality, and enacted by two personality planets, the Sun and Saturn. Mostly under the pressure of circumstances, the client had done everything in her power to avoid loss and, by doing so, had developed her personal initiative and ability to cope with life. When, at last, she was fully self-reliant and had completed her development, she was released from her various

Figure 1.5.5. The horoscope of a client whose parents divorced when she was seven years old.

anxieties. The whole process lasted from the divorce of her parents when she was seven until her forty-third year. As a rule it is possible to trace any individual development cycle by Age Point progression in this way. The process usually begins at the opposition or conjunction and lasts for thirty-six years, or half-way round the chart from the starting point, by which time the capability implied by the planet concerned will be fully developed and matured. As in the above case, consultant and client together should be able to work out all the connections. The relief shown by the client when the real causes have been uncovered is often amazing. The following instances should help to exemplify this further.

● Case Histories

Our first example chart shows a client (figure 1.5.6) who was forty-seven years old when she came for advice. She wanted to know something about her destiny and about the childhood impressions which had formed her attitude to love and to professional life. When she was seventeen (AP at 25° Taurus in sextile to the Sun/Pluto conjunction), her father fell seriously ill and she was obliged to stop training as a hospital nurse because she was needed at home.

In order to understand the part played by the father, we must look at the radical position of the Sun. The latter stands at the Low Point of the sixth house in conjunction with Pluto, in opposition to the Dragon's Head and the Moon and square Mars (to give the triangle of performance). The sixth house has always been known as the house of work and of diseases; and here we see the father, whose disease created problems affecting the native's work (sixth house). The triangle of performance indicates, however, that the native will be compensated by her father's love and appreciation for what she has done. Prior to this he had never thought of praising her, but had behaved like a self-opinionated man who always had to be right.

Saturn in the second house was responsible for her strongest childhood impression. This must have gone very deep, because it influenced her subsequent behavior. Characteristically, the events of her sixth year of life were not easy to remember, and it was only after she had been told that the experience in question had to do with her female libido and love ideal (Saturn in opposition to Venus and Neptune) that the scales fell from her eyes. Visibly moved, she related the following incident: "Yes, I was playing at being nurse to a little two-year old boy from down the road and was giving him his physical examination, when my mother [Saturn] saw what I was doing, yelled at me and snatched me away. Father, too, happened by and he smacked me for the very first time. It was horrible. I could not understand why my parents were so upset or why my father had hit me."

From this time on, her mother was always able to manipulate her by making her feel guilty, as shown in the 2/8 axis of possession. Only when she reached the age of forty-two and the conjunction of Venus and Neptune on the cusp of house eight, was she able to throw off her mother's influence. Against her mother's will, she overcame all obstacles and took a trip to India. None of her parents' expostulations or reproaches were able to deter her—she simply had

Figure 1.5.6. Horoscope of a female client born July 16, 1935, at 8:45 PM in Herisau, Switzerland.

to go. She made up her mind to climb out of her rut and to leave behind everything that stood in the way of her development. And so the eighth house challenge to make an inner change (death and transfiguration) was accepted. She had to face up to the things she had previously avoided, and endured considerable mental anguish until she had summoned sufficient strength and courage to release herself from the behavior patterns and unconscious compulsions of childhood.

In preparation for this individual development—a goal in life indicated by her Ascendant sign Aquarius—there was a transit of the Sun/Pluto conjunction at age thirty-three. She got to know a man at that time and experienced a love such as she had not thought possible. Her sense of personal worth was confirmed, not only because she was loved but because she had won the love of a man who was her intellectual and social superior. That was all to the good as far as her development was concerned, but there could be no consummation of the relationship since he was already married and did not want to hurt his wife. She had to suffer the pangs of renunciation, and this worked a change in the fundamental motivation of her life.

Pluto, with the Sun and North node (in opposition to the South node in the twelfth house), has a metamorphic power that thrusts aside false projections and modes of behavior in order to release the springs of the innermost being. What we learn from the Dragon's Tail is that the love of a man was not sufficient for complete restoration of her self-respect. As a point of ascension, the Dragon's Head is in individualistic Capricorn in twelfth house, implying that the native has to learn self-reliance and to free herself from dependence on a partner or on her environment. This development commenced at the age of thirty-four, just as the native's Age Point was entering Leo. At that time she enjoyed a busy and profitable year of learning, of travel, and of exploring her own abilities. And thus the way was prepared for the final break with her mother's influence at the transit of Venus/Neptune and the opposition to inhibiting Saturn.

* * *

Figure 1.5.7 is the horoscope of a client who expected astrological advice about her special abilities and on her chances of finding a partner. She was forty-six years old and her Age Point stood at 15°

Libra in quincunx to the Saturn/Mercury opposition. Although ready to enter a fresh field of endeavor, she felt rather helpless.

The center of gravity of the aspect formation is in the first quadrant, and the detached Saturn/Mercury opposition to Neptune along the 2/8 axis immediately catches the eye. When asked what happened when the Age Point transited this conjunction, at the age of six and a half, the client said after a moment's reflection: "My mother threw away my favorite little doll because it was old and tattered. As far as I was concerned, this doll was a part of myself no matter that it was dirty and broken. I was so attached to it that I always took it to bed with me. Incomprehensibly, it was suddenly no longer there. To me, as a child, this did not make sense. I still remember how it stabbed me to the heart. I cried all day, was unmanageable, shut myself in my room and plotted revenge. My hatred of my mother lasted for almost two years."

Figure 1.5.7. A female born on March 23, 1936, at 4:25 AM in Bern, Switzerland.

Then, came the Sun/Moon conjunction at the age of eight and a half, introducing another theme, namely a close relationship with her father. This relationship was very important to her at that time. When she was seven (with the Age Point practically half-way between Saturn and Sun/Moon) she fell behind at school and had to stay back in her third year. Her father was very supportive during this period of failure and did what he could to restore her self-confidence. Exactly at the transit of the Sun (when she was eight and a half years old) she passed into the higher grade with flying colors.

At the age of forty-three she married a man her mother could not endure. The Age Point was square Saturn and Neptune, the two planets representing her traumatic childhood experience. Her mother did everything in her power to prevent the marriage. But the greater the parental opposition, the more desirable did the man seem to the native. Later she came to realize that she had wed him to spite her mother. An opposition unconnected with the other aspects (here Neptune to Saturn/Mercury) works like an automatic mechanism and in stress situations betrays the individual into doing the wrong thing. Thus this lady wanted to pay her mother back for throwing away her doll so many years ago. But in reality she harmed herself, because she suffered a great deal during her marriage: her husband was self-centered and often brutal.

When the AP opposed the Sun/Moon conjunction at age forty-four and three quarters, she obtained a divorce, and felt as if she had escaped from a nightmare. Winning the decree was the counterpart of her success in the class examination at the time the Sun was transited when she was eight and a half.

As the above example illustrates, the Age Point will, in due course, transit both poles of an opposition and, on coming to the second pole, will frequently indicate a period similar in character to the one existing when the first pole was being transited—except that the situation is more clearly defined and, to some extent, has to do with a higher stage of consciousness.

* * *

Figure 1.5.8 is the horoscope of a female client who has the conjunction of the Sun with Pluto and Mercury on the cusp of the sixth house which turns our thoughts straight away to the client's profession. She is a social worker specializing in family therapy.

The personality planets in the sixth house are typical of an aptitude for work of this type.

The path of the Age Point is quite interesting. It transited the Dragon's Head when the native was in nursery school. To the enquiry concerning how this time had affected her, especially with regard to any anxiety or deprivation of love (opposition to Moon/ Neptune), she responded as follows: "My governess was very strict and I was afraid of her." She was asked: "Did she threaten you with anything (as seems likely in view of the fact that the opposition lies in the shadow of the 2/8 axis) or did she alternate threats with promises (since this axis suggests she probably employed the "carrot and stick" method)?" Her immediate reply was: "Yes, of course. There was something. My parents went away for four weeks, and my

Figure 1.5.8. A female client born July 30, 1949, at 9:20 PM in Zurich, Switzerland.

younger sister and I were left in the care of our governess. During this period she would often say, 'If you don't behave yourselves your parents will die.'"

No wonder the client continued to be haunted by visions of the death of her beloved father and mother! Her chronic anxiety was the reason why, with the transit of Uranus and Mars and during almost the entire passage of the AP through Cancer (age 22-26), she underwent a course of psychoanalysis. The transit of the Sun (on the sixth house cusp at the age 30) marked a very good period, which had begun with the AP entry into the Sun's sign, Leo, when she was twenty-eight. Professional advancement, popularity and success were the key-notes of this phase. Everything offered by the Leo Sun by way of strength and qualities of leadership began to shine through.

When she came for advice she was thirty-three years old (at the Low Point of the sixth house). Her visit was on account of her man friend, who was some two years younger than she, and of whom she was very fond. He was a carefree fellow, a good dancer, and he gave her plenty of what made life pleasant. Yet it was this very thing which filled her with misgivings for, having reached the Saturn/Venus conjunction, she thought that her partner ought to be a much more serious person with a strict moral code. The counsellor pointed out to her that she needed to rid herself of her illusions concerning love and marriage. Her Moon/Neptune conjunction is not far from Low Point seven and the Dragon's Tail and signifies non-fulfillment of her dreams or illusions. With Virgo straddling her cusp of partnership and with and with Saturn/Venus so close to the seventh cusp too, it was advisable for her to look on marriage as a challenge requiring her devoted attention.

Previously she had believed that her partner should be someone who met her highest expectations and that all she had to do was to wait for "Mr. Right." However, she quickly recognized her error, because she had already begun to see a glimmering of the truth. Later she informed us that she had married her friend and was expecting a child. The latter was born just as the Age Point was transiting the Venus/Saturn position.

*   *   *

Figure 1.5.9 shows a horoscope with another instance of the conscious assimilation of early impressions: between the age of eleven and twelve the native had her tonsils out. The AP had entered Aries and was transiting the Moon/Venus conjunction with aspects to Uranus, Mars and Pluto. Her mother was heavily engaged in business and was not able to spend time with the child. The latter was left in hospital and felt deserted. Before the operation she had entered a new class and the teacher did not like her. The girl was mortified by the consequent neglect.

The Moon/Venus conjunction represents an intense need for love and tenderness, and the individual wants to be loved at all costs. Her sense of harmony demands style; she does not care to associate with uncouth individuals. The love she demands is always frustrated in the end however. Being left alone as a child threw her selection mechanism out of order. Because she did not experience affection during her formative years, she attracted men who punished her by

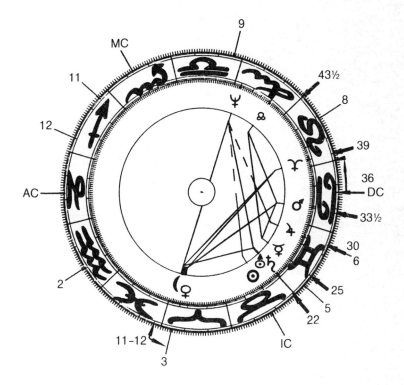

Figure 1.5.9. A female client born May 11, 1942, at 1:13 AM in Zurich, Switzerland.

either withdrawing their love from her or by becoming physically violent (Venus/Mars square). At the age of twenty-two, when the AP was close to the Saturn/Uranus conjunction, she married a childhood friend, but separated from him at age 25 (when the AP was conjunct Mercury). The marriage was contracted under the auspices of Uranus/Saturn (she was looking for security); the separation took place at the transit of Mercury square the Dragon's Head (a symbol of separation). At the transit of the rather isolated Jupiter, when the native was 30 years old, she married a wealthy man. She had a town house, a country house, and lived a life of dignity and luxury. Nevertheless, when Mars was transited (at Low Point 6, when the native was thirty-three and a half) the situation became intolerable and she divorced this man as well. Upon the transit of the DC, when she was thirty-six, she met a man-friend with whom she lived until the AP entered Leo. At this point, helped by the energy of Leo and Pluto, she came to herself. Shortly after the AP had reached the DC, she underwent a course of analysis and identified many of her YOU-fixations, illusions and projections, and freed herself from them fairly quickly.

* * *

Figure 1.5.10 illustrates another example of Age Progression. At the AP transit of the stellium in Virgo (age 9-18) this client experienced great difficulties within the family. She felt hemmed in and, although she had brothers and sisters, there was nobody in whom she could confide, nobody who took her seriously—she was alone.

The counsellor asked, "What was your relationship with your parents?"

"My parents? Oh, yes, they disappointed me. My mother, in particular, was absorbed in her own problems, and had no time for me or for my problems. Therefore, I was very much at the mercy of my environment and was tormented by guilt feelings."

"Well, it certainly looks as if what happened in your early impressionable years had a decided influence on your further development. Did you remain with your parents long?"

"Yes, until I went to America at the age of twenty-eight."

"I see. So at the Low Point of the fifth house, when the Age Point was in Sagittarius, you were finally able to break away from your old environment. But what happened to your childhood and teenage impressions? Were you also able to break free from your guilt feelings and your dependence?"

"Break free? No. It's true I had gone far away, but in myself I wasn't free; I was discontented and my guilt feelings were with me in America."

Exactly at the time of opposition to the stellium (age 46-54, when the AP was passing through Pisces), she lived through nearly seven years of severe upheaval. Having returned with her husband to the family milieu, she walked back into situations where she was not understood, just as she had not been understood as a child, and experienced the same old sense of frustration. Her self-confidence went completely. At the Low Point of the ninth house, the crisis reached its peak. Misunderstandings with relatives, financial losses,

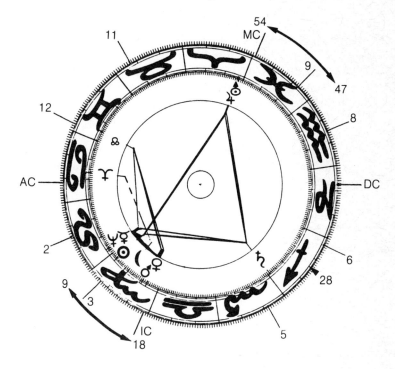

Figure 1.5.10. A female client born August 28, 1927, at 2:00 AM in Luzern, Switzerland.

conflicts with herself and with her partner all escalated. She felt universally misunderstood, lost her grip on reality and reached the verge of suicide. This was the typical crisis of consciousness and of transformation   at the ninth house Low Point, in which the individual feels that there is nothing left in life except to wander aimlessly in a kind of no man's land. Being thrown back on herself, "I AM" was the only thing to which she could cling. Eventually, after making a slow recovery, she took the decision to go abroad with her husband again.

When she came for advice, she was just turning fifty-four. After transiting the MC, the AP moved from Pisces into Aries: from the end to the beginning of the Zodiac. This invariably signifies a big change in the native's life, and we may be sure that, together, the MC and the sign Aries will help her to an inner rebirth and to a new start in life. She herself describes her existence in these terms: "My life has been full of stumbling blocks and false trails. I could never develop properly but was always the one to give and suffer. Office work did not satisfy me mentally, nor did the existence of a housewife. Life to me looked something like this: I was standing in a straight street. On each side of the street, herbs, bushes and trees were all in bloom (dreams, illusions, longings—or the real me?). Then the main road came to a dead end, but many small paths branched off it. I had to continue my journey without benefit of a signpost and without knowing the destination. The way was thorny in places; it was full of danger, and hateful and treacherous. Although my journey along it has been costing me so dear in physical and mental effort, I have not given up.... Nevertheless, I should like to return to my 'own street'—back to my better self."

Chapter 6

Life's Time Table: The Age Point in the Twelve Houses

Introduction—Age Point in the 1st House (Aries)—Age Point in the 2nd House (Taurus)—Age Point in the 3rd House (Gemini)—Age Point in the 4th House (Cancer)—Age Point in the 5th House (Leo)—Age Point in the 6th House (Virgo)—Age Point in the 7th House (Libra)—Age Point in the 8th House (Scorpio)—Age Point in the 9th House (Sagittarius)—Age Point in the 10th House (Capricorn)—Age Point in the 11th House (Aquarius)—Age Point in the 12th House (Pisces)

● Introduction

In the following section, we shall be taking a look at the lessons to be learned, and the changes and problems to be faced at the various stages of life. Examples will be used to demonstrate problem positions and unusual Low Point experiences, and thus to elucidate the application of the Age Point.

The examples have been chosen at random and are merely illustrative. They should not be treated as definitive statements. We have been thinking about the best way to represent the special influences of the Age Point without having to confine ourselves to the basic effects of one house or period of life. For a while we hesitated, knowing the beginner's fondness for generalizing specific statements, and we would beg the reader to regard the examples as no more than teaching material. Even if he should find similar positions in his own chart, he will discover that the descriptions do not fit his own case in every respect. Much depends on the sign and house in which a planet is posited, also on its aspects—and this is a very individual matter. Correct interpretation involves a consideration of the part of the house where we find the planet: cusp, pre-cuspal area, Low Point, Invert Point, etc. And when we come to the aspects, we have to look not only at the overall configuration but also at their relative tension (that is to say, whether they are red, blue, or green aspects). It is also important to note cases in which planets have only one aspect—or none at all.

• Age Point in the 1st House (Aries)
   ## Age 0-6

Development of bodily functions. Complete dependence on parents. Awakening of ego-consciousness. Stubborn phase.

During the first months and years of life, the individual is still not conscious in an egocentric sense. He or she is as yet unable to distinguish between the ego and the environment. At this stage, the child is simply there and requires love, nourishment, warmth and protection. It is completely identified with its surroundings and is therefore extremely open to the impressions that come from these. Everything encountered by the child at this time, and also the things it misses (such as tenderness and security) tend to mould its

Figure 1.6.1. An example of the Age Point in the first house and extending into the second house because of the presence of planetary stelliums.

character. Only between the second and fourth year of life (Low Point of the first house) does the child begin to experience itself as an independent being. He becomes consciously aware of his surroundings for the first time. He begins to use the word "I." Impelled by this first stirring of the ego, the child enters the so-called obstinate phase, a period alleged to last no longer than two years in normal circumstances. It may even be briefer, covering no more than the time-span around the Low Point (age 3 to 4). If the obstinate phase continues into the second house (age 6), we frequently find planetary stelliums in front of or behind the second house cusp with hard aspects, as depicted in figure 1.6.1.

When we look at the aspects in this figure, we realize it would be useful for parents or teachers to know that this child will react defiantly when pushed too hard. He wants to defend his ego against any encroachments from his environment and, if he knew how, would express himself something as follows: "Here I am, and I have every right to my little bit of living space!" Above all, when the Sun or one of the other ego planets is after the Ascendant, this is always a sign of a preoccupation with the self so strong that it conflicts with the environment.

Some parents try to break the will of such a child and do all they can to make it fall in with their own plans and wishes. They demand instant obedience without any regard to the temperament of their offspring, and their attitude is frequently mirrored in difficult planetary positions lying under the shadow of the second axis. But if a "rebellious" child is always being disciplined every time it "gets out of line," this can store up trouble for later in life.

The better parental response is one of patience, which will be fortified if a glance is thrown at the AP to see how long the clash of wills is likely to last. In this, the strongest phase of ego-formation, the child normally begins to define its own living space. According to the dynamic theory of the houses, the second house influence starts to be felt at the Low Point of the first house when the native is three and a half years old. The child tries to file a claim it can defend against those with neighboring claims. This is the first constructive, social reaction of the EGO. At this crucial juncture the child becomes aware that other people also have personalities and that they too have staked out their claims.

Figure 1.6.2 on page 136 shows yet another approach to this phase. Saturn near cusp two and square the Sun in the collective

Figure 1.6.2. Another example of how the Age Point indicates stress that may affect future development.

area is usually an indication that the child has to win some of the living space owned by the family or by its father or mother. This creates an underlying anxiety that its own right to be one of the family might be in jeopardy, and could set a life-long pattern of defensive behavior—even when there is no longer any reason to be apprehensive. The individual always seems to be saying: "Halt, who goes there? This is private property." The first really effective method is then that of the second house: making one's own estate, one's own living space.

● Age Point in the 2nd House (Taurus) Age 6-12

Psychic development. Making one's own living space and habits. The distinction between "yours and mine." Ownership crises.

At the age of ca. six, the child begins to have his or her own possessions in the true sense of the word, and guards them like costly jewels. If anyone else presumes to touch them, there may be a sharp reaction. The real value of an item does not enter into consideration. Perhaps it is a broken car or a doll without arms or legs, but that does not matter—it is enough that the doll or car is the property of the child. Nobody has the right to throw an old doll away, "It is *my* doll!"

It is a serious mistake to clear out the child's toy-box during this formative period, or secretly to throw away its old bits and pieces while it is at school. By so doing, one shatters the basis of trust.

A typical example is an opposition along the second axis, or a performance triangle. From the planetary placement in the second house (or for that matter in the first or third houses) the exact timing of the formative experience can be calculated for the period between the ages of six and twelve. (For further information refer to Impressions of Early Childhood on page 117.)

Each unwelcome intrusion on the child's living space and sphere of possessions has an effect on the development of the ego. Its possessiveness is related to a sense of personal worth, and its typical "second house behavior" will determine the subsequent attitude to ownership. Parental admonitions against being a 'dog in a manger,' or continual hindrances put in the way of the child having its own property, usually lead to compensatory behavior in the adult where goods and chattels are concerned; to the extent perhaps of pathological envy, greed, cupidity and food mania, or of over-reactions against these such as asceticism, posing as an enemy of private ownership, etc.

This is the age at which children enjoy playing inside a small wigwam or house made of plastic sheeting. The game is all part of the process of securing living-space for the "I" in which it can shut out the interfering "YOU." Behavior learned now is most significant for later social deportment. Preoccupation with creating and maintaining one's own little environment clearly lessens at the Low Point (age 9-10). Of course, it does not disappear entirely, for everything we experience leaves its mark and becomes a part of our character, but its influence on conduct slowly fades.

When there is a planet under strong tension situated at the Low Point of the second house, especially if it is one of the ego planets (Sun, Moon or Saturn), the position of the child becomes awkward as soon as the Age Point reaches this position—at the age of ten years in figure 1.6.3. on page 138. Its struggle for possessions, living-space and protection does not meet with the same success as formerly. With this placement, the child is unlikely to receive much affection from its mother, and its situation does little to boost its self-confidence. In fact it is instinctively aware of becoming too set in its ways to the detriment of its general performance. Not that the realization is put in so many words; it is more in the nature of a deep but very positive feeling. Generally, at the Low Point of the second house (between the ages of 9 and 10) the environment is experienced as more powerful than the self.

Now it is true that the second house is not an angular house like the first, the Low Point of which (equivalent to the age of 3 and a half) introduces the obstinate phase; nevertheless the theme of this succedent house does undergo a comparable change in spite of its greater "fixity." The child recognizes that it must make a greater effort to enter into positive relationships with its environment. It has to learn that it must give in order to get. The difference between "yours and mine" begins to be understood. During this learning process it gravitates towards the cadent third house. The latter is not an activity house in the true sense of the word, but a house of discovery, perception, observation and experience. The child becomes increasingly interested in such possibilities during the period between the second house Low Point and the third house cusp (between ages 10 and 12). Hence that period is known as the "learning age."

For the first time in its life (at age 10 at the earliest), the child starts to learn of its own accord, and its classwork shows a marked improvement. It wants to find out as much as possible about everything and to understand what other people know. The child looks on those around it as cleverer than itself and therefore superior. Since it wishes to become one of these clever people, it tries to discover as much as it can about the world. That is the main

Figure 1.6.3. Planets under strong tension in the second house create problems with self-confidence early on.

reason for its eagerness to learn. What is more, the child enters puberty during this period and starts to take an interest in the opposite sex. In a way, this is a special form of the same principle: the individual wants to know and understand. And so the classical learning time in the intellectual sense begins at the third house.

An accurate analysis of the signs and planets occupying the space between Low Point Two and Cusp Three is particularly important if proper decisions regarding the child's education are to be taken—decisions having far-reaching consequences for its future life and profession.

● Age Point in the 3rd House (Gemini) Age 12-18

Development of the emotional and intellectual functions. The age of puberty; ambivalent shifts of mood. Idealistic notions, development of the will.

At the age of twelve—on the cusp of the third house—the young person enters the region of collectivity (houses three and four). The chief urge at this time of life is to be accepted into the community. The growing person begins to feel the urge to take wing from the confining family nest and to soar into the comparative freedom of society at large. The search for a wider community is led by idealism and accompanied by cricitism of the settled order (the family). The more strongly the family is identified with the standards and morals of the establishment, the more liable is the young person to have the feeling of being misunderstood and even "let down" by relatives. He or she looks for like-minded friends outside the family; and, in fact, groups of young peers with shared interests are easier to find in today's world than ever before. Many parents wring their hands over the fact that in this age of mass-communication (fast cars, the press, radio and TV etc., all closely connected with the third house) the family unit is less well able to cope with the competition from the street than it was some decades ago. A change is necessary in our educational methods too, if we are to keep pace with the altered conditions of modern times; blind authoritarianism has to yield to a more sympathetic understanding of the spiritual development of idealistic youngsters.

Between twelve and eighteen, children start using abstract thought. They try to absorb as much information as possible or have it crammed into them by their teachers or lecturers. Lessons are learned and the students are regularly tested, but their approach is piecemeal and frequently they fail to appreciate the bearing of one fact (or branch of knowledge) on another. Not before the LP of the third house at the earliest (15th to 16th year of life), and more often not until the age of eighteen, do young people begin to see the wider connections. This is the time for going to college or starting work training. What is being learned now is more vital and more related to other things. The next house (house four) is a water house, and, as it is approached, emotional qualities take the stage: the thinking is no longer purely cerebral but is enriched by a significant deepening of the emotional life At this age, the young person often displays an intense interest in philosophy or sociology, and in religious or political questions. For the first time, he or she may wonder if the world is really as it should be, and may enthusiastically espouse new ideas for changing it. Doubts concerning and criticism of the establishment can lead to revolutionary activities, from joining student protest movements to getting involved in terrorism.

When the native has Mercury or Saturn in the third house, as shown in figure 1.6.4, and Mercury or Saturn is square to Jupiter and in opposition to the ninth house—forming a thought-axis-based efficiency/performance triangle (traditionally the T-square) with its apex pointing to the "opposite number," the "YOU"—it is particularly important for the native to "stick to his or her guns"

Figure 1.6.4. An aspect configuration showing the need to stick to ideals to get free from surrounding influences.

and not to let the thinking be dictated by those around. When there are planetary stelliums in the third house, those around will do their utmost to manipulate the young person into a "safe" situation where he or she will soon conform to the wishes of society. When this happens, the idealistic notions are usually abandoned pretty quickly.

The tendency of collectives to level their members arises from a natural desire for security and protection on the part of society, so this is normal, but it doesn't make the person who owns the chart very happy.

If there is an opposition along the thought axis, i.e, from the third to the ninth house as shown in figure 1.6.5, this always implies a confrontation between the collective way of thought and the personal world-view. The individual wants to emerge from the common herd and to rise superior to it by saying "No" to its dictates. When the Age Point makes contact with this opposition, the resistance of the environment will be experienced; he or she will feel misunderstood, and, in extreme cases, threatened by society. Conversely, by being disruptive or heretical, they may spread unrest. In school, especially, such trouble-makers face determined efforts to make them knuckle under quietly. Whether or not they can be made to do so will depend on the sign on and the planets in the third house. Even at this age, the conformists may be distinguished from those who think for themselves. The latter must reckon on always having to stand alone; for the interests of the two types are naturally very divergent.

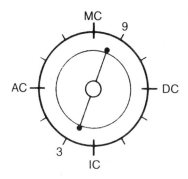

Figure 1.6.5. An opposition on the 3/9 axis shows a conflict between our goals and behavior.

When the LP is reached between age fifteen and sixteen, there is increased conscious awareness of sexual differences; and with it comes a conflict between the mind and the emotions that is profoundly unsettling to the adolescent, and often productive of considerable fluctuations of mood.

The period between sixteen and eighteen is also a difficult one for the parents. The young person is approaching the IC, the individual 4/10 axis, and wants to stand on his or her own two feet and to strike out an independent line. To most parents this is a thorn in the flesh, since they hope to keep control of their child and to choose its pathway through life. At this time they often find their children's behavior thankless; the children refuse to say where they have been or what they have been doing. It is hard for the parents to see the children slowly slipping out of their control. The adolescents come home to eat and sleep and that is about all. They feel compelled to "try their wings" and to get out and about in the world. It is best for parents to be very understanding at this time. In spite of everything, the children cannot be expected to be sufficiently mature to enter the struggle for existence on their own without suffering character damage. For the time being they are full of ideals, but these will have to be tested against the hard realities of life.

● Age Point in the 4th House (Cancer) Age 18-24

Separation from the parental home and traditions. Opting for one's own emotional attachments and affiliations. The tendency to "get up and go."

By the eighteenth birthday, the crisis of puberty is practically over. Due to the development of the sexual function, the parents should be appreciated more as adults, as man and wife, than as elders. An urge toward independent growth springs up in the teenager, who becomes aware that he or she is an individual with a taste for freedom. Until now, any sense of individuality has been rather hazy.

Figure 1.6.6 shows an opposition on the individual axis (4/10 or IC/MC). Each opposition on the individual axis joining the fourth and tenth houses indicates strong individual endeavor. If it crosses another opposition on the 3/9 axis, the native often clamors for personal freedom, wishing to break free from the common herd and, when the Age Point makes contact with this position, will want to brush aside all restrictions without more ado in order to pursue the most appealing course of action. Another possibility is that a sudden bid for power or fame will be made, especially when there is an ego-planet like the Sun or Saturn in the tenth house.

The fourth house signifies (for a young person) the effort to find a suitable place in society, offering a certain degree of status and room for action. With this in mind, he or she will try to join a congenial group of people. This personal group could be a football club, university, church or trade union, but, whatever the case, the motive will be enjoyment of a shared interest.

In general, the young person at this stage will turn more and more from the family; abandoning the old collective and identifying with one of his or her own choice or, if choice is out of the question, joining one that happens to be available.

When the LP of the fourth house is reached (age 21-22), the young adult begins to display a definite desire to leave home, inspired by a sense of the propriety and importance of possessing a place he can call his own—situated in some preferred locality. For various reasons (the length of time spent in vocational training being one of the most significant of these nowadays) this desire is not always so easy to fulfill. However, at the very least, the young

Figure 1.6.6. Oppositions create restrictions and a need for growth when the Age Point goes through the fourth house.

person ought to be provided with private living space (a room of their own) to be decorated and furnished as they wish, his or her creativity and longing for freedom being given as much scope as possible to manifest and unfold.

Figure 1.6.7 illustrates a fourth house heavily tenanted by the personality planets Saturn, the Sun, and Moon, and the parents may fail to comprehend these natural instincts, and may even have repressed them. When the Age Point transits these positions, traumatic processes of separation can be set in motion or relationships with father and mother can turn sour. If the aspect shape is a closed one or a so-called "bowl" (as in figure 1.6.7), the dependence can be so great that it clips the native's wings so to speak. Frequently the environment will hinder the development of self-determination.

At the latest after the LP has been reached in the fourth house and while the ascent is being made to the cusp of the fifth house (age 22-24), the young adult ought to have learned to take charge of life, to trade punches with the world when necessary, and not to creep nervously under the parental roof for protection. Parents whose children have so far failed to make their own way in the world, should seriously think of "stirring up the nest" a bit. It is important at this age to become a founding member of one's own group. Formerly this was achieved by marrying and having children. Today, the young sometimes gather in communes during the period the AP is transiting the fourth house.

Figure 1.6.7. Age Point in the fourth house involving Saturn, the Sun and Moon.

● Age Point in the 5th House (Leo)
Age 24-30

Autonomous phase, progress in professional life and in building a family, love matches, creative self-development.

The fifth house is the most adventurous of all the houses. It is the house for proving oneself in the world, and involves contacts with the many individuals who cross our path. They and we are thrown together in the hurly-burly of life, and sometimes these confrontations (with the YOU) can prove to be extremely fruitful. The animated scene is often full of fierce struggles, with cut and thrust on both sides; hard knocks given and taken are all part of the learning process, which is not always easy. During this period of life, we are extraordinarily expansive and think we can conquer the world at one stroke. Such behavior is right and proper at this age, since it enables us to measure our capabilities against reality. More or less consciously, we discover our limitations.

Planets in the fifth house indicate special experiences at this time of life. If Saturn, the planet of restriction, is there, the native will be restrained or uncomfortable in his or her contacts. Things do not run so smoothly as with the Sun or Moon for example. If, on the other hand, either of the libido planets (Mars or Venus) is there, the love life will be strongly activated during the Age Point transit. (See figure 1.6.8.)

Figure 1.6.8. Planets in the fifth house indicate an important phase when the Age Point passes age 24-30.

In the fifth house, corresponding to the sign of Leo, it pays to be jovial and magnanimous in true leonine fashion; then we shall gain the hearts of our fellow-men and -women. Also, we shall learn the extent to which people can be won over by sympathy and liberality, incidentally discovering the strength and scope of our powers and how far we can go. In the process, a clearly defined form of behavior emerges by which we may well express our personality for most of our life. We become marked out by our bearing, our gestures, our clothing, and by our approach to people and things.

The planets in the fifth house have much to tell us about this. With Venus we easily win folk's sympathies. With Mars we are inclined to be too direct, too brusque. With Jupiter we are jovial, but invariably know how to take our advantage. With the Sun we can sway others. With Saturn we like to impose conditions, either consciously or unconsciously.

The period covering the ages from twenty-four to thirty is a very intensive phase. The potentials of the planets and the signs have to be worked out in actual experience where they will be hemmed in by reality. When the AP arives at the Low Point of the fifth house (age 27-28), a measure of failure is evident. The Low Point is particularly prominent in every fixed house, since the principle of fixity comes strongly to the fore. By analogy, the fixed house we are now considering has many of the qualities of Leo, and its Low Point makes itself distinctly felt. Anyway, we are cut down to size by people and things, and in the process come to know ourselves better. There is a risk that we shall be brought low, but may also climb to a new vantage point where vistas of hitherto hidden knowledge (not generally associated with the fifth house) will unexpectedly burst upon our gaze.

With the transit of the AP over one of the three spiritual planets Uranus, Neptune, or Pluto, we are likely to be brought into contact with religious movements, or with mind-changing ideas introduced to us by certain books or individuals.

In some respects, the Low Points of the houses on the right of the chart are the key to the opposite houses on the left. Thus the LP of the fifth house can represent our approach to the eleventh house. With planets in the eleventh house and an aspect pattern on the 5/11 axis, ideals will assume importance quite early on. Careful reflection should yield significant insights at the LP and help us to find the true balance between outer and inner reality. Individuals of this age frequently display intense interest in the spiritual side of life and

Figure 1.6.9. When the Age Point moves through the fifth house and touches aspects to Uranus, Neptune, or Pluto, the individual makes important changes.

its problems, especially if one of the spiritual planets is involved in any transits or aspects the AP may make. By so doing they have an opportunity for creative self-improvement and can enjoy the highest the fifth house has to offer. To some extent, all of us sow seed in the fifth house for a harvest to be reaped from the eleventh house between the ages of sixty and sixty-six. Whatever house is being transited, it is worthwhile looking at the axes, because one house sets the stage for another, and by allowing for this fact we can see the relationship between a given age sector and the whole chart. See figure 1.6.9.

● Age Point in the 6th House (Virgo)
Age 30-36

Adjustment phase. Defensive life situation. Vocational crises. Mastering existence. Incorporation into the community.

If the fifth house is a dominant, active house, the sixth is subservient and passive—corresponding to the serving sign Virgo, so unlike ruling Leo. This difference comes out clearly as the Age Point crosses the boundary between the two houses: from the positive, even aggressive attitude to the world, there comes a retreat into suffering and endurance. We are thrown on the defensive—especially where the LP is located at the age of 28.

From an existential point of view, we each have to find our slot in the market place when the Age Point is passing through the sixth house. As seen by society, each of us has something to offer in the way of output or capability: some creative talent. We each possess personal qualities worthy of being developed in the situations into which we have been born. The task before us is to find our unique niche; a task that seems to become more urgent during this period. Now is often a time for refresher or re-training courses to enable the native to give of his or her best or to gain job satisfaction. Finding the right job or profession demands a very subtle play between skill and will, between wishes and possibilities. We have to place a realistic value on what we can do and we have to present it properly, demanding neither too much nor too little. Finding the happy medium is the task of the sixth house.

The sixth-house planets suggest how we shall have to exert ourselves and what requirements we shall have to satisfy. With the Sun or Pluto, for example, we shall possess the fund of vitality necessary for performing arduous tasks. We may even go in search of such tasks in order to prove ourselves. With Venus, Jupiter or the Moon, we are much more tractable and allow ourselves to be influenced or unsettled by our environment.

During this period of life, we must see how we can explore the options open to us in the light of our abilities. This is most important, as it guarantees, confirms and secures not only our outer but also our inner existence. Lack of success can lead to acute crises, especially in late starters who have yet to find their true path, for

Figure 1.6.10. When the Age Point passes through the sixth house, natal oppositions may cause a crisis relating to self-support.

these people are ever searching and experimenting, and may already have abandoned one or more careers (perhaps due to setting their sights too high). This is the time to abandon all plans that are not in keeping with the personality. There the great uncertainty experienced by individuals who have so far failed to put their lives on a firm basis may easily be imagined.

Especially where there are hard aspects (oppositions) along the 6/12 existence axis (see figure 1.6.10), and even more strongly when two oppositions cross, problems to do with existence keep on recurring. As the Age Point transits such a position, a desperate crisis can arise affecting the very core of the being. The native's self-esteem may be shattered and he or she may be plagued by extreme doubt, thinking, "I'm good for nothing," or "Nobody wants me around, I'm no use to anyone," and oscillating between pity of self and bitterness against the world. The upshot could be full-blown depression, antisocial behavior or some form of psychosomatic illness.

There is always a danger of slipping into some form of disease in crises of this sort. If we snap under the strain, an inner despair may result which will cause us to be whisked away into a twelfth house situation—the twelfth house signifying, among other things, hospitals. We may wonder whether we are able to handle life and whether, indeed, life makes any sense at all. Here again the Low Point (age 33-34) is an essential factor in setting a new course. The individual may suddenly realize that the wrong profession has been chosen and so he or she will apply for retraining—the sixth house being closely associated with further education. For, because it shares many of the characteristics of Virgo, it presents us with opportunities to redress errors affecting body, mind and vocation. This is the house in which we concern ourselves with health matters, the cure of disease, and also with social duties. The problems of life are best solved by caring for others. "In helping others, we help ourselves," is the appropriate maxim for this house and this period of life.

And so, in the sixth house, one can set about making sure that one is in the right job or profession, not only for the sake of earning a living but for the sake of inner contentment. If, for example, as shown in figure 1.6.11 on page 150, there is a trine between Uranus (or some other planet) in the sixth house and the Sun or Jupiter in the tenth, and if a third planet forms with these trined planets a so-

Figure 1.6.11. Planets in the sixth house can also inspire an active career when the Age Point moves here.

called big blue talent triangle, the chances are that either we know quite early on what we want to do in life or, when the Age Point transits Uranus, we become energetic enough to enter on a career in keeping with our abilities.

● Age Point in the 7th House (Libra)
   ## Age 36-42

Formation of new connections, revision of life-style, partnership problems, life changes, high point of personal development.

When the seventh cusp is reached, a rather successful time begins. It is true that the influence of the sixth house very often continues for a further year or thereabouts, but generally speaking the effect of the seventh house starts to be noticed before the cusp.

Whatever the cusp, some sort of stress situation is encountered just prior to Age Point transit. We have the feeling of having to climb a steep mountain. Especially with the cardinal axes 1, 4, 7 and 10, the going is particularly strenuous. We experience an intensification of external and internal forces urging us on. Again and again, events start to snowball or we are drawn into matters beyond our control.

After the seventh cusp has been passed, success may suddenly be achieved on our own terms. Our chances for "being ourselves" improve; we get along better with our opposite numbers and are accepted for what we are. This is the theme of the seventh house. Now we can link up with those who are able to help our development: especially if Jupiter, Mercury, Venus or the Moon occupy the house. New paths can open up without any special effort on our part. Suddenly the realization hits us: "This is the way for me—this is the direction I can take!" Quite often the new decisions taken at this time are professional; but usually it is our personal relationships that take on a new aspect, since the seventh house is the house of partnership.

As the seventh cusp (the DC) is transited at the age of thirty-six, we enter the conscious sector of the chart. Since this is the day-time sector, we see many things in a fresh and clearer light. Factors that formerly over-influenced or troubled us can suddenly disappear. We can awake like Sleeping Beauty to things that until now we have not perceived or considered, whether they are external events or inner realizations. The process is one of becoming consciously aware, not only of ourselves but also of our partners. Such a process frequently has its painful side, particularly when we have lived under the spell of big illusions concerning partnership, spouse or contacts. Shortcomings on the part of our partners and ourselves are now found to be excessively disturbing. We can no longer tolerate or ignore them. There is also the chance that our partner will start finding fault with everything, and the shared life we have taken so much trouble to build up will no longer mean anything to him or her. Quite severe matrimonial crises can arise, usually lasting until the Low Point (40 years of age).

If an encounter axis joins the "I" with the "YOU," *i.e.*, if there is an opposition involving the first and seventh houses (see figure 1.6.12 on page 152), disappointments could mark the passage of the Age Point through the seventh house. Should the majority of planets be on the "I" side, we shall be too much inclined to impose our own personal ideas and wishes and too little inclined to make due allowance for those of others. Acute crises in marriage or partnership should result in differences being clarified or ironed out, and should bring fresh insights. With an opposition on the I-YOU axis it is difficult, however, to distinguish the different elements and to recognize the real cause of the crisis. We can not clearly see how and to what extent we make projections on one another. Consequently, we are amazed when we suddenly recognize that our partner thinks, feels, and behaves quite differently from the

Figure 1.6.12. When the Age Point moves through the seventh house, it is a real encounter should planets be involved in an opposition between the seventh and the first.

way we have always assumed they did. In this confrontation of the I and the YOU, what matters is a mature, concerned relationship enshrining a nice balance between sharing and freedom of action. It is necessary to be constantly aware that both of these have contributed to the forming of the relationship and that both will determine its outcome. Perhaps there will be a separation or divorce. If a divorce is decided, several years will have to elapse before the process is complete, which will usually be at the Low Point (age 40) or even at the cusp of the eighth house (age 42).

Nearly all of us begin to entertain doubts as the Low Point is reached (between the ages of 39 and 40), wondering whether pulling together or 'go-it-alone' is the best policy for us. This incipient uncertainty can have the most varied causes. If, for example, the Age Point transits Uranus in the seventh house, and Uranus is involved in hard aspects from other planets, as shown in figure 1.6.13, the longing for personal freedom will be accentuated. The native will start thinking along such lines as, "My situation has become too stifling. I need to be myself again; I shall have to secure more room for my own development." With other planets, Neptune or Venus say, we are simply tired of our obligations. In which case, we look for a little bit of immediate freedom, and resort to various sly tricks to obtain it. With Saturn under difficult aspects in the seventh house, and especially when it is at the Low Point, we may find that our partner cannot be tied down. We must learn to give them their freedom even when it hurts to do so.

Figure 1.6.13. Uranus in the seventh house, for example, may force a relationship to re-evaluate itself when the Age Point moves through the seventh.

Another reason for crisis is the appearance of the first signs of the onset of old age in the form of certain small infirmities which can no longer be dismissed. The hassle and wear and tear of life are beginning to take their toll, although we are still not prepared to admit it.

● Age Point in the 8th House (Scorpio) Age 42-48

Change of life-style, death and transfiguration, social status, making sure of life.

During this phase of existence we are concerned firstly with stabilizing our position in society, and secondly with turning our attention to spiritual things. We feel the need to bestow some thought on the good of our souls. It is helpful if we can use our achievements to date as a sort of "fly-wheel" to keep us "ticking over" comfortably. Now is a time for drawing on our reserves and for reaping the benefit of former efforts; so that we can devote more time and energy to cultural, spiritual or philosophical pursuits. This fixed scorpionic house has long been associated with in-heritances, legacies and the possessions of one's "opposite number." Therefore the transit through the eighth house is a period in which we receive what we have earned—or get our just desserts. It is not unlikely that we shall be offered various positions in society, if we have gained a reputation for reliability. On the other hand, past frivolity and carelessness may lose us financial and social status now.

Because of the strong instinct for self-preservation, it is a natural reaction at this time to cling to what has already been accomplished, to fight against change, because we want security in the roles we have grown used to playing. But if we dwell too much in the past and persist in trying to re-enact the scenes of yesterday, we shall succumb to the death-and-transfiguration process of this Scorpio house. What has just been said almost seems like a contradiction, yet it lies in the nature of the transformation process that everyone has to undergo in one way or another during this period. Our passage through the eighth house forces us to adjust to the realities of life; we need to protect the roots of our life certainly, but also to grow spiritually. If we fail to do the latter, our materialism and clinging to dead forms will be purged by losses of all kinds. The things to which we are holding on so tightly will be snatched away from us. Our old world will suddenly crack wide open so that a new one may hatch out. In this connection it is interesting to note that the Low Point of the entire zodiac falls in the sigh of Scorpio (12-½ degrees). The name so often given to the eighth house—the house of death—would seem to find its explanation here. At this time of life we frequently lose things on which we have bestowed considerable love and care. Our parents may die, our children may leave home, or we may find ourselves stripped of some

Figure 1.6.14. The passage of the Age Point through the eighth house will inspire an individual to try something new.

favorite office or function. Those who have applied themselves to building a career abandon it without warning or they break out of their familiar circle.

Eighth house crises have two main causes: in the first place we are seeking the path to the MC (the individualization point) and ever more independence and personal freedom, yet feel hemmed in by living conditions and the social set-up, or by the strong will of our partner. In the second place we may have to recognize that we made a mistake in our younger days and allowed ourselves to be guided too much by what the group thought and did. Now we are consumed by the desire to regain our liberty but are hindered by a hundred obligations and restraints.

Figure 1.6.14 illustrates an individual who has a performance triangle touching the 8th house, and the Age Point transit begets a wish to throw the past to the winds in order to take up something new. Usually we have allowed ourselves to be manipulated by life (or by our environment) into a fixed situation, but are now aware that we can no longer keep treating this as a passing phase. One possible reaction to this insight is resignation. We lose our last, fine illusions concerning how special we are, concerning our prospects of un-trammelled liberty or free love, and at that point we just give up. The reaction need not be negative. Instead of resignation we can assist at the birth of the spiritual person. Giving up or letting go are really no more than a change in life's motivation, a renewal in the spiritual sense. They are psychological counterparts of the eternal theme of death and transfiguration, and will help us achieve an inner rebirth during the so-called midlife crisis.

Here we have considered one manner in which the eighth house can be experienced. The reader may experience it entirely different-ly. Personal development has much to do with the case, and with whether the crisis affects the material, mental or spiritual side of life. Also, the signs occupied by the planets, and the part of the house in which the latter are posited (on or before the cusp, at the Low Point or Invert Point, etc.), all have a hand in this; as does the way in which these planets are involved in the aspect configuration.

An instructive example from our own practice is that of a young man who encountered a powerful aspect configuration just on the cusp of the eighth house when he was turning forty-two (see figure 1.6.15 on page 156). During the run-up to the eighth house, near the Low Point of the seventh house (age forty or therabouts), he felt completely trapped and looked on his whole existence as a prison from which there was no escape. He was unable to respond like a normal person to contacts and became neurotic. A defense mechanism had been formed when the Moon was transited around age ten, and it had interfered with his life for thirty-six years while the Age Point was traversing the empty space. Not until the opposition could the diverted vital energy break through. This demonstrates how serious such a life crisis can be.

As the Age Point reached the Saturn/Uranus conjunction, the young man attempted suicide because he was living at loggerheads with his father, his mother was dead, and a love affair (transit of Venus) had just ended. His world lay in ruins around him and he lost the will to survive. What had happened? What was the cause of his breakdown?

Figure 1.6.15. The chart of a male client who experienced a major transformation during the Age Point passage through the eighth house.

As a little chap of ten or eleven, just as the Age Point was transiting the lunar pole of the Moon/Mercury opposition, he had had his homelife disrupted by the war. The Moon-ego of childhood, with its need for love and security (2nd house) was replaced by a super-ego based on the fight for folk and fatherland. This was out of keeping with the child's nature, but helped him to come to terms with his fate as it was at that time. He continued to wear the same mask of bold confidence in the eighth house when he felt unable to cope any longer.

At this juncture two things happened. First he went back to his old job as a printer, and then—and this is what brought about the most far-reaching change—he became devoted to a mature older woman who mothered him and lent him her psychological support. She understood him and helped him to start a new life with her. What happened bears all the marks of the eighth house. He died to himself and was "reborn." That death is also rebirth is a lesson worth remembering in the time of crisis, if we are to move on confidently to the ninth house cusp.

● Age Point in the 9th House (Sagittarius) Age 48-54

Acceptance of greater responsibilities for the community, instruction of others, construction of a world of spiritual values, or else a sudden inability to make sense of life with resignation.

In this house of the expansion of consciousness (Sagittarian in character) we have the opportunity of taking up new and fascinating interests. We may well start delving into philosophy, religion or esoteric matters, start pondering the meaning of life or make a pilgrimage to some strange and distant shore, our choice being governed by the signs and planets in the ninth house. If we have managed to disengage ourselves from unnecessary tasks over the preceding few years, we shall now have more time to spare for the things we really want to do. The period between the forty-eighth and the fifty-fourth year of life is the so-called philosophical phase. Here it is wise to start occupying ourselves with the essential values and realities of life in preparation for the onset of old age.

At this time, we shall discover that the external world is not the be-all and end-all; worldly success, power, riches and fame may help to make life more settled and secure, but do not guarantee a fulfilled and happy life. The loosening of old ties in the eighth house has already been leading to this conclusion, but the ninth house brings it into clear view. And so there is an opportunity to see things in a new and more independent way.

Like the other cadent houses, the ninth is associated with questions of meaningfulness. We ask ourselves, "What is the meaning and purpose of my life? How best can I serve humanity?" Back of these questions is a desire to make sense of the whole workings of creation: the mind broaches philosophical and transcendental matters. Personal interests are no longer paramount. Actually, we should be bestowing our attention on problems of this sort as early as the Low Point between the ages of forty-four and forty-five, for if we do not we run the risk of coming to a dead-end in the ninth house.

Figure 1.6.16 shows ninth house planets in opposition to planets in the third house, so the native's opinions will not always be in line with the opinions of the group. This conflict will in fact already have arisen. If the opposition is aggravated by being part of a projection triangle (*i.e.*, of a triangle incorporating an opposition together with two long green quincunx aspects and a sextile), the Age Point transit can provoke a spiritual crisis, similar to the "Faustian" struggle for the ultimate truth, in which we are seized by a gnawing doubt.

Figure 1.6.16. Planets in opposition in the third and ninth houses can force a crisis when the Age Point moves through that house (age 48-54).

The uncertainty crisis over the meaning of life as the Low Point of the ninth house is reached at the age of fifty-two, detaches us from the tried and trusted. We enter a so-called "null-sphere" where we should let go all egocentricity. In letting go, however, we are caught up to where our field of vision is widened to see things in their true proportions. This is in keeping with that saying of Socrates, "Wisdom begins only when we know that we know nothing."

As with Low Point transits in any other house, a new orientation is required here too. So many things appear to make no sense and we ask ourselves what the use is of all our knowledge and other accomplishments if we cannot pass them on. In this crisis it can be helpful to return to the ideals we had during the third-house period at age twelve to sixteen. As life widens out again we shall gain courage and renewed motivation.

When houses are above the horizon, it is always wise to take a look at the periods of the houses beneath them. The functions of two diametrically opposite houses, one above and the other below the horizon, are complementary. (See figure 1.6.17.) The poles of the axes are related in quality to a certain extent, and one house is the shadow of the other from whichever end we regard them. Each end makes its own contribution sooner or later.

In order to continue to enjoy life in the ninth house, we must leap out into the spiritual, into the transcendental—rather like a parachutist making a jump into the ocean of air. By so doing we gain the necessary distance from our little egos to operate more effectively. Since we are no longer so closely identified with events,

Figure 1.6.17. Opposite houses are complementary and one house is actually the shadow of the other.

we can work for the well-being of the whole. Especially when the Age Point is transiting the region of the Low Point, we have a chance to extend this distance and to behave more impersonally.

During the crisis of trying to make sense of life, and when there is a strong drift towards resignation, an opposition from Saturn in the ninth house along the thought axis can cast that planet in the role of "the dweller of the threshold before the spiritual gates." Saturn is a personality planet and as such represents the protective space surrounding the ego. For this reason, it is reluctant to release whatever it happens to be holding. But the ninth house demands expanded awareness and an abandonment of effete standards before we proceed on our way.

With Saturn in the ninth house (see figure 1.6.18) in opposition to the Sun in the third, it is not easy to place personal ideas and wishes in the service of the higher, ethical aims. At the Low Point at ca. fifty-two years and just before the M.C. at ca. fifty-three years when Jupiter is posited there for example, it is particularly important to see oneself set against the spiritual background of life as a whole. One will not then be so full of self-importance, but will make an effort to understand and help the rising generation and to accept the new world and advance with it. This tolerant attitude is essential for further development.

Figure 1.6.18. With Saturn in the ninth house, it is not easy to allow oneself to grow spiritually as the Age Point passes, but it is necessary to further development.

● Age Point in the 10th House (Capricorn) Age 54-60

Authority and individuation phase, identification with the calling, fulfillment of life's expectations, ossification.

Here too, as in angles four and seven, the impulse imparted by the MC (the 10th house cusp) is experienced as a strong incentive to be independent. At the age of fifty-four we have reached the highest point in the chart, where we and the world stand level. We see ourselves as we really are, and that is how we have to present ourselves. There is no longer any room for self-deception; we are obliged to show ourselves in our true colors. If we have something to offer, some skill or specialized knowledge, we shall be entrusted with greater responsibilities. It is impossible to hide behind others any more, and if we try to do so Fate will probably give us "a shove in the back" to force us into the open.

In the tenth house, the house of individual flowering, we have independent authority and the development of an inner vocation. Here is the place where experience and maturity can prove their worth. If the ripening process promoted by the ninth house has been successful, the native will find himself endorsed by his group around the time the MC is being transited. The group perceives that the native knows what he is talking about, that he is competent, and is therefore prepared to trust him with some of its affairs.

And so it often happens that people enter public life at this time, perhaps after previous attempts to do so have proved abortive. This usually occurs when a planet is not so powerfully placed in the tenth house (middle to Low Point)—but is now able to exert its influence.

Figure 1.6.19 on page 162 shows that this is true even of planets in the shadow of the axis: for example, Jupiter or some other planet just in front of the MC with the Sun in the tenth house on the Low Point. With an aspect formation predominantly on the ego-side, the native may never have obtained proper recognition, but now, with a transit by the Age Point the world suddenly sits up and takes notice of him. With this position, the individual does not strive for fame but endeavors to cultivate the ability indicated by Jupiter or one of the other planets. In which case, the motive is self-fulfillment not the pursuit of power.

Figure 1.6.19. Jupiter in the shadow of the MC.

The period of life between the ages of fifty-four and sixty should be one of fulfillment if our special qualities are able to come to fruition. The environment often encourages this without any forcing on our part; the time is a particularly happy and satisfying one in which we reap the reward of past exertions. Yet here too there are problem positions requiring our attention.

Figure 1.6.20 shows an opposition along the individual axis from the fourth to the tenth house. Someone also having a stellium in the tenth house (especially one involving hard planets) can indicate tragic experiences or reverses at this time. If wrong means have been employed on the road to power and prestige, if corners have been cut unfairly, or if vaulting ambition and the lust for power have led us to kick others aside, we shall be repaid in the same coin when the Age Point makes its transit, and as likely as not will be rebuffed by those around us. Every sham authority that has not grown organically will be questioned and may be overthrown; every false claim on the service and respect of our fellows will be rejected sooner or later—at the latest when the tenth-house Low Point is reached.

Near the Low Point, in the fifty-eighth year, our juniors often begin to be seen as rivals. We become nervous of losing the position so dearly won and for some time oppose every internal and external change. The Low Point of house ten represents an important turning point in life. Standing, so to speak at a corner, we cast a backward glance on an active professional life, and also look ahead to a period when we shall need more rest for lack of energy or enthusiasm to face the hustle and bustle of the workaday world. As

Figure 1.6.20. An opposition from the fourth to the tenth.

yet we do not know how we are going to shed our responsibilities or how we shall spend our new-found leisure. Our maturity is now put to the test—a maturity which does not depend on any outward success, but on integrity, inner strength, and creative imagination. Many a time we shall be shaken and shall need to fight to keep our balance, not so much by preserving our outward poise as by clinging to spiritual principles, inner values and experiences.

The tenth house is in a certain sense the last house of worldly joy. Already with the transit of the MC we have quitted the right side of the chart. All the energies flowing to us from close association with our fellows are on the ebb. Whoever wears the chain of public office in the tenth house may discover that he becomes progressively isolated and that his private life is affected too. For the most part, those who engage in public activities suffer an erosion of their private lives. They are under constant observation and cannot do just what they like.

• Age Point in the 11th House (Aquarius) Age 60-66

Digestion of life's experiences, ethics and tolerance, new friendships and relationships—or isolation and resignation.

The eleventh house usually brings with it a noticeable decline in contacts as compared with the number of contacts made from the fourth to the eighth house. At this time of life it is best to confine oneself to a small circle of friends, and to a few deep relationships. The years spent in the eleventh house from 60 to 66 are also suitable for taking stock. In the "more rarefied atmosphere" of the house corresponding to the air sign Aquarius, we are usually elevated above the world's feverish activity. This is the time to enjoy a more comprehensive view of things. For example, many people start writing their memoirs now, perhaps in a late bid for fame, although the main motive is to crystallize the essence of life's experiences. The years stretch back into the past. For a long time the native has been working hard to secure a good position and a comfortable retirement, and can now ease up. He will reflect on how insignificant his troubles often were, and on how often he squandered his energies on things that seemed important at the time but were really of little moment. Lessons are learned which would not have been understood twenty years earlier. The native also discovers that often it was not others who deceived him: he deceived himself by taking it for granted that his affairs were bound to develop in a certain way.

Here, then, is an opportunity to acquire a degree of wisdom, to see past mistakes in a clearer light, and to recognize what has to be altered and improved. Perhaps a circle of friends is formed for the exchange of opinions. A decision has to be made: since it is no longer possible to serve humanity in general, the native seeks out the people with whom he has something in common, people with whom he can share his thoughts and experiences, and deepen his philosophy. Contacts with youngsters tend to improve, because the individual is no longer fighting to keep ahead in life and has shed much of his dogmatism. There is an understanding of the problems faced by the young—who are always willing to accept advice given in a spirit of tolerance.

With one of the sensitive planets, Neptune, Jupiter, Venus or the Moon on the eleventh cusp, and this person will usually intuitively know who will form the most reliable friends. It is certainly important in the eleventh house, the house of friendship, to make friends who are genuine: not acquaintances who are there only when the going is good, but folk prepared to give loyal support during a crisis. When sensitive planets occupy the eleventh house, the native most likely had a good attitude towards others, even in youth, and will therefore be surrounded by loyal friends even at this stage—and will probably not suffer loneliness. To attract and keep friends, we need ethical behavior, kindness and a sense of fair play.

In the phase of life represented by the eleventh house, we generally wish to place our experience and our practical wisdom at the disposal of others, and so long as this is done with the right motives and in the right way (that is to say with a desire to be helpful without being condescending) others will profit by it. One of the most useful tasks of this period is to rid ourselves of one-sided ideas. If we fail, we may end up alone and friendless!

At the Low Point of the eleventh house, around age sixty-four, folk commonly discover that many of their acquaintances are no longer interested in them and even try to avoid meeting them. Their friends desert them; especially their younger friends, who somehow seem to be too busy to see them. Perhaps they have to face the deaths of old comrades—always a painful experience. Health problems or crises are also fairly frequent around Low Point eleven. Retirement lies just ahead, and this in itself can give rise to depression and anxiety. The less initiative the person has, the more he or she will be gripped by the fear of loneliness and old age. Failure to overcome the "little me" syndrome will leave the native with no road forward into a fulfilled life. If, by the time he has reached the eleventh house, he still has not shaken off the shackles of "poor little me," he will suffer from hypersensitivity. The least sign of neglect will mortify him deeply. He will stalk away sulkily and will cut himself off even from good companions; in which case there can be a negative crystallization of self-assertiveness in this fixed house, perhaps accompanied by senility.

Figure 1.6.21 on page 166 illustrates the possibility of counselling someone with a red square in the fixed houses 2, 5, 8, 11 or oppositions from hard planets like Pluto, Mars, Uranus or Saturn along the 5/11 axis. Health problems of some serious concern regarding friendships will undoubtedly occur. Usually, the problem is that the mind has lost its flexibility. Not all the fitness training, flashy ties, or showy hats in the world can magically restore the verve of youth. Endless stale reminiscences become a terrible bore to the listeners. And the causes of these things are usually to be found in earlier periods in the fixed houses.

In this connection, we should also mention the numerous causes of "pensioner's collapse." Individuals who have expended all

Figure 1.6.21. A chart showing a grand square in the fixed houses. The Age Point passage through the eleventh house will be very important.

their energies on the struggle for existence but have neglected to cultivate pursuits suitable for their old age find themselves suddenly out on a limb, not knowing where to start. Therefore it is extremely important to make preparations in the fifth or (at the latest) in the eighth house, for the big change to come.

Nevertheless, the eleventh house can also prove very enjoyable if we have the chance to be ourselves once more and possess the health and strength to spend our time well. This will bring fulfillment to us and will benefit those around in the bargain.

● Age Point in the 12th House (Pisces) Age 66-72

Completion of life, gradual cessation of personal effort, voluntary withdrawal or one forced by illness, self-finding.

The twelfth house is the last in the full circle, but this does not mean that life ends here; it merely closes the round. In keeping with its nature it produces a return from the outer world to the core of self. By the Low Point of the eleventh house at the latest (sixty-three and a half) we should begin to realize the meaning of this phase of life. As we already know, the Ascendant is the symbolic ego point in the chart, and its attractive power is felt as soon as the MC is transited. That is why the pivotal theme and task of the twelfth house is the return to the center of oneself. A certain isolation is required for this task and, if the native will not seek it of his own free will, nature will provide it for him.

Figure 1.6.22 shows a stellium of hard planets in the twelfth house (e.g. Saturn, Mars or Pluto with squares and oppositions). When this configuration exists, it often happens that the native is isolated at this period of life, being packed off to an old folks home, or abandoned by his family to live in a lonely room. The twelfth house theme is that of detachment from the external world to turn inwards for the purpose of exploring our own inner dimensions. The person who has passed through the earlier stages "correctly" will have no trouble here, but may anticipate a gracious old age, a time which enables him to see clearly both himself and the relationships between inner and outer. It will also be a time of gratitude for everything that has been experienced in the past and may yet be experienced in the future, of thankfulness for the riches of adventure and knowledge life has brought.

Since, in the twelfth house, we have little or no dealings with the world at large, it is possible to sit and meditate on self and the universe. We can become more detached since life has become much less demanding. The conditions are ideal to turn to higher things and to discover the treasures within; to learn how to be alone with ourselves.

After the Low Point, we enter the expansive sphere of the ego and the pull of the Ascendant can already be felt. In this phase from

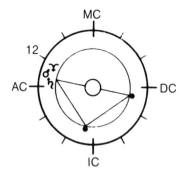

Figure 1.6.22. A stellium in the twelfth house shows mostly isolation in this life period.

age 70-76 (LP to LP) we are required to find our true selves and to become self-sufficient. This necessitates a release from everything external that would imprison the self, in order that a higher condition of soul may be born from the center of the being. At this juncture, a split is experienced between the wish to sit back and savor the ripe fruit of achievement and the impulse to forget the joys and sorrows of the past in order to embrace life again like a newborn and carefree child. The result is often a spiritual rebirth which will carry the life far over the Ascendant again, or else will produce mere second childhood. Unpleasant symptoms of aging, such as senility and physical degeneration, are retarded and even avoided by a mentally sound, vital attitude. Acceptance of life, the joy of living, affection, and sensible body care all contribute to an intact ego which will still function well physically in the twelfth house. If, in addition, we are free from everyday pressures, from the struggle to keep the wolf from the door, from obligations and debts, we can adopt the spectator's role and have fun joining in the game of life on the sidelines. For preference, the pensioners should not be solitary, but should remain in circulation and be given a quiet window seat from which to watch the world's comings and goings. And so the individual remains lively and awake; as, in fact, we see in Mediterranean lands, where old people sit at the window or in front of the house; they do not say much and usually are not conspicuous, but they share in everything going on around them, they study the world and their expression is one of content.

Figure 1.6.23. A well-aspected Sun in the twelfth house may inspire new creative potential when the Age Point passes through.

It the Sun is well-aspected (see figure 1.6.23) in the twelfth house and the whole aspect picture is framed by the fourth quadrant, natives may not realize their full potential until they are old. They will still be needed, perhaps as grandfathers or grandmothers. Grandparents are often good teachers, since they are able to pass on their experience. They are standing at the necessary distance from life and can offer the children understanding, whereas younger educators tend to project their own conceptions and compulsions to the children. For another thing, grandparents and grandchildren are pretty close to one another, because the elderly have an emotional rapport with the young.

With the transit of the AC (age 72) we are new-born in a certain sense, and receive a jolt of vitality something like that received at birth. Astrologically speaking, we have a new and quite conscious perception of any planets posited in the first house. We recognize dimensions which, although they are familiar to us, look new in the light of seventy-two years of earthly existence. When these planets were being transited in our infancy, we were in a passive position with regard to our environment and were not free to take our own decisions. There was no possiblity of digesting and working on all our impressions. But now, in our old age, we meet these planets again and have an opportunity to use this fresh encounter to reach a deeper understanding of our destiny and of ourselves. A good example is available in the life of C.G. Jung, and in Part Two of this book we shall be describing in detail the Age Point Progression of his horoscope.

PART II

Example Charts

Chapter 1

Age Progression in the Horoscope of C.G. Jung

Introduction—Description of Jung's life—C.G. Jung's birth chart with the most important Age Point data—Aspect structure in Jung's chart—The Leo Sun—Relationship with father and mother—Age Progression and life rhythm—Astrodata Age Progression Tables—C.G. Jung's Age Progression and Course of Life.

● Introduction

The following astrological study of the Swiss physician and psychologist Carl Gustav Jung (1875 to 1961) is offered as an example of the manner in which the AP can be used in practice. There are several reasons for the choice, the first being that Werner Stephan, who researched the Progression of the Age Point in the horoscope of C.G. Jung for us, has been involved in Jungian depth psychology for many years and so is a very reliable source of information on Jung's life work. In addition to studying his writings, he has prepared a didactic analysis of analytical psychology and has also been in contact with various individuals who knew Jung personally.

In his study, Werner Stephan has concentrated on the most significant periods in Jung's life and has worked as far as possible with verifiable data. Obviously, limitations of space prohibit reference to more than the salient facts, and therefore just a few periods of the great man's life have been sketched in—deserving though they are of fuller treatment. Werner Stephan has wisely placed the main emphasis on the Freudian period and on the following interim period, which are very revealing of Jung's thought and give the reader a deep insight into his understanding and into his system of analytical psychology.

● Description of Jung's Life*

In order to obtain as objective a picture as possible of the life of C.G. Jung, it is indispensable to read the book about his life: *Memories, Dreams, Reflections*. The reader will then be able to judge how Jung's preoccupation went hand in hand with whatever problems were currently being posed by the Age Point. The likenesses are amazing, even when no attempt is made to exaggerate them or to overrate their significance.

One of the chief reasons why I have chosen the life of C.G. Jung as an example of Age Point progression is that in Jung we have a man who, as a psychologist and psychiatrist, turned his attention on the inner life and had a unique gift for writing about the world of the soul. Now we know that the movement of the Age Point mirrors the movement of the inner, psychological life and is only indirectly suggestive of outer events; yet it is very difficult to garner adequate data on the interior life of famous people. Most biographies concentrate on external happenings and achievements, drawing a veil over what went on in the person's mind. Jung, quite exceptionally, made a point of stressing the significance of his inner experiences; so he meets our need perfectly. He said of his life that fate would have it that all the "outer" aspects of his life were accidental. Only the interior proved to have substance and a determining value for him. Eventually the memory of outer events faded, and he said that those "outer" experiences were never very essential, and when they were it was because they coincided with phases of inner development. Much of the "outer" manifestations of his life vanished from his memory—for the very reason that he participated in them with all his energies.[1]

---

*Contributed by Werner Stephan.
[1]C.G. Jung, *Memories, Dreams, Reflections*, edited by Aniela Jaffe, Pantheon Books, NY, 1961, p. ix.

Jung goes on to say in the *Prologue* to his autobiography that he was only concerned with his inner experiences, as these are the ones that he remembers best. Because he felt this way, and was willing to write about these experiences, we can easily study the course taken by Jung in his life and the path of the Age Point with its associated inner psychic attitudes and motivations.

Before taking a closer look at the Age Point progression, I want to present a brief study of Jung's natal chart, since this will show us the key to understanding the Age Point. Especially would I draw the reader's attention to the aspect pattern governing the native's motivation, for a knowledge of his motivation is indispensable to any attempt to interpret what the Age Point might trigger.

The aspect formation in Jung's natal chart (shown in figure 2.1.1 on page 176) falls into three main patterns or figures: Pattern 1 is a large trapezium formed by the planets Pluto, Jupiter, Mars and Saturn. The inclination of the trapezium to the Ascendant reveals the strong tendency to introversion in Jung's life, especially in youth and old age. Pluto in conjunction with the Moon serves as a point of contact with Pattern 2.

Pattern 2 is a scissors figure composed of the Moon, Uranus, the Lunar Nodes and Venus/Mercury. This is a clue to Jung's other and contrasting personality style, namely his Leonine readiness to star on the world's stage. Finally, Pattern 3 is a detached Sun/Neptune square embraced by the scissors constellation. This square underlines the worldly nature but with the accent on dependence: recognition and positive feedback were vital to Jung and he was liable to be sharp with his critics. Also in this square we see his obvious feeling for transcendence: that equivocal aspect of his personality, which can neither be defined nor completely understood. What is more, the difficult relationship with his father has its basis here.

Presumably it was these different personality styles which induced the biographer P. J. Stern[2] to diagnose schizophrenia in Jung (supposedly cured through his own individuation process). According to our chart, there was no split in the personality styles, and according to Jung, an interplay between personality styles is normal to the growth of the individual. A constant interplay

---

[2]P.J. Stern, *C.G. Jung: Prophet des Unbewessten* ("Prophet of the Unconscious") R. Piper & Co. Verlag, Munich, 1977. (Publisher's note: As far as we know, this work is not available in English.)

Figure 2.1.1. The horoscope of Carl Gustav Jung, born July 26, 1875, at 19:20h in Kesswill, Switzerland. This chart includes the most important Age Point dates that we will be discussing in the text. The reader should know that another birth chart exists for Jung, based on a birth time corrected to 19:32h. This may be found in the chart collection titled *Meine Begegnungen mit C.G. Jung und Hermann Hesse*, by M. Serrano, Rascher-Verlag, Zurich, 1968. (Publisher's note: We do not think this volume is available in English.)

Table 2. Astro-Data Age Progression for C.G. Jung

Date	Day	Aspect	Body	Date	Day	Aspect	Body
1875 Jul	27	HC	1	1886 Jul	28	□	☿
1876 Jan	27	□	♆	1886 Sep	17	△	☿̇
1876 Feb	**13**	☍	☉	1886 Oct	19	⚼	☾
1877 Jul	8	✶	☋	1887 Jan	25	□	♀
1877 Nov	9	⚻	☿	1887 Jul	27	HC	3
1877 Nov	10	IP	1	1887 Aug	2	△	♂
1878 Jan	11	☍	☋	1887 Dec	7	⚼	♈
1878 Feb	20	□	☽	1887 Dec	27	☍	♃
1879 Feb	14	✶	♂	1888 Jan	17	✶	♄
1879 Apr	11	LP	1	1888 Dec	27		☋
1879 Jun	23	□	♈	1889 Jun	25	☌	♆
1879 Jul	11	△	♃	1889 Jul	11	□	☉
1879 Aug	**4**	☌	♄	1889 Nov	10	IP	3
1880 Jul	22		♓	1890 Nov	24	⚼	☋
1881 Jan	22	✶	♆	1891 Mar	25	✶	☿
1881 Feb	8	⚻	☉	1891 Apr	12	LP	3
1881 Jul	27	HC	2	1891 May	25	□	♀̇
1882 Apr	26	⚼	☋	**1891 Jul**	**4**	☌	☾
1882 Aug	3	△	☿	1891 Nov	1	✶	♀
1882 Sep	22	⚻	☿̇	1892 Jun	18	⚻	♂
1882 Oct	24	✶	☽	**1892 Oct**	**24**	☌	♈
1883 Jan	31	△	♀	1892 Nov	10	⚻	♃
1883 Aug	7	□	♂	1892 Dec	3	□	♄
1883 Nov	11	IP	2	**1893 Jul**	**27**	**HC**	4
1883 Nov	13	✶	♈	1894 Mar	17		♅
1883 Dec	3	⚻	♃	**1895 Apr**	**8**	⚼	♆
1883 Dec	22	⚼	♄	**1895 May**	**12**	✶	☉
1884 Sep	28		☋	1895 Nov	11	IP	4
1885 Feb	25	⚼	♆	1897 Apr	11	LP	4
1885 Mar	8	△	☉	1898 Apr	16	✶	☋
1885 Apr	11	LP	2	1898 Dec	31	⚼	☿
1886 Apr	**20**	☌	☋	1899 May	12	✶	☿̇
1899 Jul	27	HC	5	1917 Jan	22	△	♆
1899 Aug	3	⚼	☾	1917 Feb	7	⚼	☉
1900 Mar	17	⚼	♀	**1917 Jul**	**26**	**HC**	8
1901 May	**26**	☍	♂	1918 Apr	26	⚻	☋
1901 Nov	10	IP	5	1918 Aug	3	✶	☿
1902 Jan	20	⚼	♈	1918 Sep	8	⚼	☿̇

Table 2. Continued.

Date				Date			
1902 Feb	22	△	♃	**1918 Oct**	**22**	△	☽
1902 Apr	8	△	♄	**1919 Jan**	**31**	✶	♀
1903 Apr	**11**	LP	5	1919 Aug	7	□	♂
1904 Jan	18		♋	1919 Nov	11	IP	8
1904 Dec	24	✶	♆	1919 Nov	18	△	♈
1905 Jan	23	⊼	☉	1919 Nov	30	⊼	♃
1905 Jul	**27**	HC	6	1919 Dec	2	⊼	♄
1907 Mar	**11**	□	☊	**1920 Sep**	**28**		♎
1907 Sep	**5**	☌	☿	1921 Feb	23	⊼	♆
1907 Nov	11	IP	6	**1921 Mar**	**8**	✶	☉
1907 Dec	5	⊼	⚸	**1921 Apr**	**11**	LP	8
1908 Feb	1	✶	☽	1922 Apr	20	☍	☊
1908 Jul	**27**	☌	♀	1922 Jul	28	□	☿
1909 Apr	**11**	LP	6	1922 Sep	16	✶	⚸
1909 Jul	**2**	⊼	♂	1922 Oct	18	⊼	☽
1910 Jan	4	✶	♈	1923 Jan	25	□	♀
1910 Jan	30	□	♃	**1923 Jul**	**27**	HC	9
1910 Mar	5	⊼	♄	1923 Aug	2	✶	♂
1911 Jul	26		♌	1923 Dec	6	⊼	♈
1911 Jul	27	HC	7	**1923 Dec**	**24**	☌	♃
1912 Jan	27	□	♆	1924 Jan	17	△	♄
1912 Feb	**27**	☌	☉	1924 Dec	26		♑
1913 Jul	**8**	△	☊	1925 Jun	25	☍	♆
1913 Nov	9	⊼	☿	1925 Jul	11	□	☉
1913 Nov	10	IP	7	1925 Nov	10	IP	9
1914 Jan	**11**	☌	⚸	1926 Nov	23	⊼	☊
1914 Feb	**20**	□	☽	1927 Mar	24	△	☿
1914 Jun	23	⊼	♀	1927 Apr	11	LP	9
1915 Feb	14	△	♂	1927 May	25	□	⚸
1915 Apr	11	LP	7	1927 Jul	3	☍	☽
1915 Jun	23	□	♈	1927 Nov	1	△	♀
1915 Jul	11	✶	♃	1928 Jun	18	⊼	♂
1915 Aug	4	☍	♄	**1928 Oct**	**23**	☍	♈
1916 Jul	**21**		♒	1928 Nov	9	⊼	♃
1928 Dec	3	□	♄	1949 Nov	10	IP	1
1929 Jul	26	HC	10	1950 Jan	11	☍	⚸
1930 Mar	17		♐	1950 Feb	20	□	☽

Table 2. Continued.

Date				Date			
1931 Apr	8	⊼	♆	1951 Feb	14	✶	♂
1931 May	22	△	☉	1951 Apr	12	LP	1
1931 Nov	10	IP	10	1951 Jun	23	□	♈
1933 Apr	11	LP	10	**1951 Jul**	**11**	△	♃
1934 Apr	16	△	☊	**1951 Aug**	**4**	♂	♄
1934 Dec	31	⊼	☿	1952 Jul	22		♓
1935 May	12	△	⊕	1953 Jan	22	✶	♆
1935 Jul	27	HC	11	**1953 Feb**	**8**	⊼	☉
1935 Aug	3	⊼	☽	**1953 Jul**	**27**	HC	2
1936 Mar	17	⊼	♀	1953 Apr	26	⊻	☊
1936 May	**26**	♂	♂	1953 Aug	3	△	⊕
1937 Nov	10	IP	11	1953 Sep	22	⊼	⊕
1938 Jan	19	⊼	♈	1953 Oct	24	✶	☽
1938 Feb	22	✶	♃	**1954 Jan**	**31**	△	♀
1938 Apr	7	✶	♄	1955 Aug	7	□	♂
1939 Apr	11	LP	11	**1955 Nov**	**11**	IP	2
1940 Jan	18		♅	**1955 Nov**	**18**	✶	♈
1940 Dec	24	△	♆	1955 Dec	3	⊼	♃
1941 Jan	23	⊼	☉	1955 Dec	22	⊻	♄
1941 Jul	26	HC	12	1956 Sep	28		♈
1943 Mar	11	□	☊	1957 Feb	23	✶	♅
1943 Sep	5	☍	☿	1957 Mar	8	△	☉
1943 Nov	**10**	IP	12	**1957 Apr**	**11**	LP	2
1943 Dec	**5**	⊼	⊕	**1958 Apr**	**20**	♂	☊
1944 Feb	**1**	△	☽	1958 Jul	28	□	☿
1944 Jul	**27**	☍	♀	1958 Sep	17	△	⊕
1945 Apr	11	LP	12	1958 Oct	19	⊻	☽
1945 Jul	1	⊻	♂	1959 Jan	25	□	♀
1946 Jan	3	△	♈	1959 Jul	27	HC	3
1946 Jan	29	□	♃	1959 Aug	2	△	♂
1946 Mar	5	⊻	♄	1959 Aug	7	⊻	♈
1947 Jul	26		♒	1959 Dec	24	☍	♃
1947 Jul	**27**	HC	1	1960 Jan	17	✶	♄
1948 Jan	27	□	♆	1960 Dec	27		♈
1948 Feb	13	☍	☉	**1961 Jun**	**25**	♂	♆
1949 Jul	8	✶	☊	1961 Jul	11	□	☉
1949 Nov	9	⊼	☿				

between an outer personality (No. 1) and an inner personality (No. 2) is discussed by Jung, for he said that the play and counterplay between personalities No. 1 and No. 2, ran through his entire life, and had nothing to do with a "split" or dissociation in the ordinary medical sense. He further states that it is indeed played out in every individual.[3]

The Leo Sun

Jung's powerful Leo Sun is described very aptly in *Words and Image*, by Professor Adolf Portmann. He said that to get to know Jung, and to experience this man, was a great honor. Jung's mind was incessantly productive—to watch him grasp new insights was an incredible process. Meeting over the course of ten years at the Eranos conferences, Jung appeared as a powerful natural force, a person who had an extraordinary capability of brining out a spiritual way of functioning in all those who attended the meetings.[4]

Nevertheless, Jung's personality also had its dark side. Without doubt, the Leo Sun gave him an appetite for power and, through the isolated square to Neptune, an allergic reaction to criticism whether justified or unjustified. His arrogant nature brooked no contradiction. The emotional side of his make-up, characterized by the Moon at the Low Point (LP) square to Uranus and with Pluto near by, was blunt and irascible and from time to time expressed itself in a devastating tirade directed against his children, friends or even patients. The placement at the Low Point made these reactions puzzling and unpredictable to those around him. However, his quick mind (Venus/Mercury conjunction in the 6th house) re-interpreted the outbursts as a "necessary part of becoming conscious or of therapy."

Relationship with father

A few words are in order here about the father-and-son relationship as indicated by the detached square linking the Sun and Neptune. This position indicates that the father was out of touch with the life of the child, paying him scant attention and probably often thwarting him. To Jung, his father seemed more like a part of

---

[3]C.G. Jung, *Memories, Dreams, Reflections*, edited by Aniela Jaffe, Pantheon Books, NY, 1961, p. 45.
[4]See C.G. Jung, *Word and Image*, edited by Aniela Jaffe, Bollingen Series XCVII:2, Princeton University Press, Princeton, NJ, p. 187.

the outside world than one of the family (Sun on the Descendant) and, of course, his father's calling as a minister of religion must have had something to do with this.

In *Memories, Dreams, Reflections* we read that between the ages of 17 and 19 he had engaged in many intense discussions with his father on religious questions, but that these had been unable to dispel his nagging doubts.[5] Because his father, although a parson, was tormented by an inner conflict of belief from which the church was unable to save him, Jung's mistrust of theological thought was stirred up even more and he was confirmed in the decision to turn away from theology and to take up medicine and natural philosophy. Nevertheless, these early religious questions and doubts haunted him throughout his life and were laid to rest only in his last works (*e.g.*, in the *Answer to Job*).

In January 1896 came the premature and unexpected death of his father. Jung was 21 years old (AP in the fixed sector between the IP and LP of the 4th house) and was only a year into his medical studies in Basle. His father's death left the problems of their relationship unresolved until it was relived and integrated in his connection with Sigmund Freud, 19 years his senior (when the AP reached the Sun, as we shall see).

The death of his father is not indicated by any direct aspect from the Age Point, although the theme of the fourth house (through which it was passing at the time) has to do with relationships within the family, and especially with the parents. The transit of the Low Point of the fourth house will always loosen the ties to the parental home. The death of Jung's father set this process in motion. Since the father's death occurred without any direct pointers from Age Point aspects, we may surmise that inwardly Jung had already severed himself emotionally from his physical father.

This does not mean that Jung did not grieve for his father, or that he was through looking for a "father image" that he could relate to—it merely means that his father's death was not a terrific "jolt" to his psyche.

Relationship with mother

Jung's relationship with his mother, who, in her role as teacher and protectress is represented by Saturn, was full of problems, too,

---

[5]See *Memories, Dreams, Reflections*, p. 91 ff.

though these were rather more concrete than were those occasioned by his Neptunian father relationship. In *Memories, Dreams, Reflections*, Jung discussed an experience with his mother when he was twelve: she always called after him to give him advice when he was invited out somewhere—saying he should give his parents' best regards, he should wipe his nose, wash his hands, etc. He was bereft of self-confidence by the time he reached the house he was to visit, and refused to carry his parents' regards, or he became shy, losing self-confidence, feeling unworthy, and becoming timid. In his forlorn states, he would have to draw upon the energy of his "other," the No. 2 personality, in order to overcome the lack of confidence his mother unwittingly engendered in him.[6]

Students should read this passage directly from *Memories, Dreams, Reflections*, as it will give insight into Saturn in Aquarius in the first house for an image of the mother; the embarrassment he felt from his mother shouting after him in the streets indicates the AC in Aquarius, the Sun in the DC with Venus not far away. When he was overcome by the power of the people he was to visit, and became timid, he was reacting to Pluto square Saturn, and the Mars in Saggitarius sextile Saturn influenced his feeling insignificant when he made his contact at the house he was to visit by ringing the bell.

Taking the horoscope as a whole, I should like to lay emphasis on the Plutonian fear of the Collective with its powerful establishment, a fear which engendered obstinate resistance (Mars sextile Saturn) and kept Jung hacking out new paths for himself (Mars in Sagittarius) right down to extreme old age. In the process, traditions (Saturn in Aquarius) were studied, attacked and, if possible, overthrown (Mars in the eleventh house, the natural house of Aquarius ruled by Saturn).

● Age Progression and Life Rhythm

Let us now make a closer examination of Age Progression. Life, seen and unseen, is governed by inherent rhythms causing it to flow from one pole to the other. We breathe in and we breathe out, we sleep and wake, in the same pattern as that of night and day of ebb-

---

[6]See *Memories, Dreams, Reflections*, p. 26.

tide and flood-tide. The whole natural world around us is established on such rhythms or, shall we say, runs by such "internal clocks."

As explained in earlier chapters, our psychic life itself is guided by inner rhythms according to a preset plan. This idea of cycles in the psychic life, has to some extent already been mooted and described by Jung for he described how, in childhood, our consciousness progressively emerges from the great undifferentiated stream of life into a state of illumination and a sense of personal power. Our objectives in this first half of the life-cycle are those of finding a niche in society, and of seeing what we can accomplish in the workaday world.

Then in mid-life—which Jung also puts at the age of 36—the mature psyche gradually changes direction. The outer world with its aims, dreams and wishes slowly retires to be replaced by confrontation with fundamental questions springing from higher sources in the being, questions concerning the meaning of life, concerning birth and death, and concerning growth and maturity. The second half of life is the road back to the realm of the mother; a road back to death—which may be regarded as a new birth into life on the other side.

This basic rhythm of the psyche's development, given here in its ideal form, seldom proceeds so smoothly, and this can give rise to many neuroses. Exaggerated introversion in teenagers can segregate them from the outside world and push them into isolation; older people sometimes grow so materialistic that they become fossilized and impervious to the higher frequencies of life and wisdom.

According to Jung, extroverted individuals have an easier time in the first half of life, but are severely tested in the second half when they see death approaching; introverted individuals, on the other hand, suffer considerably in the first half of life from the lack of understanding in the world for their dreams and phantasies, but get on better in the second half.

The Age Progression Method developed by the Hubers provides a key to the study of this psychic rhythm in fine detail and helps us to detect something of the laws behind the course of human fate. The reader is now invited to trace the movement of the Age Point in the horoscope of C. G. Jung and to compare this with Jung's own words. A prior knowledge of his life and works will certainly be very helpful; to those who are unfamiliar with them I would recommend

Jung's autobiography, *Memories, Dreams, Reflections,*[7] for here he speaks freely of what went on inside of him during the growth process—something very important to understand when using the Age Point. Jung's *Word and Image*[8] shows us a great deal about his professional life, so you can use this material to also understand the events of his life. Some readers may prefer to read the horoscope details straight through, so as to get the feel of how Jung's life unfolded, and then go back to see how it appeared in the Age Point Progression, Table 2 on pages 177-179.

● Age Progression and Course of Life of C.G. Jung

The exact dates of the Age Point as calculated by the Astrodata computer (see the Age Progression Table on pages 177-179) have been placed in bold type in the text, whereas dates of the "actual" events just appear in the text.

● Age Point in the 1st Quadrant (Age 0-18)

Childhood and youth

Jung was born on July 26, 1875 at 19.20 hrs in Kesswil, Switzerland and when he was only six months old (**2/1876**) the family moved to Laufen near Schaffhausen by the Falls of the Rhine. Some four years later came another move (**Aug. 1879**), this time to Klein-Hüningen near Basel. On each occasion the related aspects (opposition Sun and conjunction Saturn) indicated that these early changes of residence created in Jung a certain lack of confidence in the security of the family nest.

In the spring of 1886 (**4/1886**) Jung entered the secondary school in Basel. The conjunction with the lunar nodes appears to

---

[7]C.G. Jung, *Memories, Dreams, Reflections,* edited by Aniela Jaffe, Pantheon Books, NY, 1961. Also available in paperback in the U.S.A. by Random House, and in the U.K. by Collins Publishers.
[8]C.G. Jung, *Word and Image,* edited by Aniela Jaffe, Bollingen Series XCVII:2, Princeton University Press, Princeton, NJ.

show here that the commencement of this new phase of life was accompanied by ambivalent feelings, and his memoirs confirm this. At this time he wanted very much to take refuge in his "No. 2" personality, which had so much to offer for the future.

The whole period was marked by the awakening of the conscious ego-personality, accompanied by dreams, day dreams, intuitions, and confrontations with the disagreeable outer world.

Until the age of 16 (**July 1891**) the No. 2 personality held a certain priority, but this was gradually lost to the No. 1 personality in a change of direction (**Oct. 1892**) coinciding with the conjunction with Pluto. What is more, the Age Point entered the shadow of Cusp 4 (**1891-92**) at that time (near the individual axis 4/10), and this introduced the theme of individuation and of thinking for himself— a development that found its outlet mainly in the study of philosophy. As the Age Point made its way from the Moon to Pluto (**1891-91**) there was a conscious awareness of what had previously been experienced in a more visionary manner and between the age of 16 and 19 (from LP 2 to Gemini with transit of the Moon) he said that the fog of his dilemma slowly lifted, and the depressive states of mind gradually improved. His No. 1 personality emerged more distinctly, while increased knowledge took over his world of intuitive premonitions. In order to develop more systematically, Jung read an introduction to the history of philosophy to get an overall view of everything that had been thought in the field.[9]

• Age Point in the 2nd Quadrant (Age 18-36)

From medical student to head physician

The No. 2 personality certainly displayed an interest in religion, philosophy, paleontology and history, whereas the No. 1 (or everyday personality) was interested in science. As No. 1 came to the fore, Jung commenced the study of medicine. He said that as the tensions of this moral conflict increased, No. 2 personality became more and more doubtful and distasteful, and he could no longer hide this fact from himself. He tried to extinguish No. 2, but could not succeed

---

[9]See *Memories, Dreams, Reflections*, p. 68.

with that either. He could forget No. 2 in school or while keeping company with his fellow students, but as soon as he was alone, the interest in such philosophers as Schopenhauer and Kant and "God's world" would return.[10]

In April of 1895 (**AP April 1895, as well**) he successfully passed the school-leaving examination (**sign change into Gemini**) and took up his medical studies and was soon initiated into the "Zofingia" fraternity, where his Leo nature began to shine (**May, 1898, AP sextile the Sun**).

● Age Point in the 5th House (Age 24-30)

At the end of 1900, Jung completed his studies and joined the Bürgholzli University Psychiatric Clinic in Zurich as an assistant (**May 1901**).

With the **transit of the AP over the Low Point**, an important event occurred in Jung's life: on February 14, 1903 he wed Emma Rauschenbach, whom he had known in his youth and who at one time had rejected him. The fact that LP 5 (**April, 1903, LP 5**) was strongly involved indicates that Jung must have been laboring under strong internal pressure. Jung solved the problem posed by the intimate side of partnership at this time by making a hasty marriage.

Perhaps the fact that this marriage was contracted under an unusually strong inner complusion was the deeper reason why his relationship with his wife Emma, except in the early years when Emma respected her husband as if he were a father, grew increasingly difficult and stormy (cf. what is said about T. Wolff on p. 190). After a while Emma became more of a saturnian, sheltering mother-figure, while the other side of womanhood—that of the seductive mistress—was embodied for Jung in T. Wolff.

Now Jung set out (**July 1905, Cusp 6**) on the long road of professional and social advancement. In August, 1905, the Age Point reached the cusp of the 6th house. The two-year phase in the shadow of the 6th cusp gave way to a period of break through. In H. F.

---

[10]See *Memories, Dreams, Reflections,* pp. 74-75.

Ellenberger's book, *The Discovery of the Unconscious*,[11] we read that 1905/6 was a very fortunate period for Jung. First, he was appointed head physician; second, he was put in charge of the out-patients department, in which there were greater opportunities for him to cultivate his interest in psychotherapy; third, the University of Zürich conferred on him the position of private unsalaried lecturer. External good fortune of this kind can attend us at the 6th house cusp, if we have worked hard to earn it.

At this stage, Jung seemed assured of a secure career as a physician and lecturer and of an equally secure, if average, financial future. That Jung's life took a rather different turn, we own to another man who had already been blazing a trail in Vienna and was striving for recognition of his revolutionary theory: the nineteen years senior Sigmund Freud.

• Age Point in the 6th House

Sigmund Freud, the fatherly friend

Owing to the early rupture in the father-and-son relationship Jung still had an open psychic wound which needed healing. He seemed already to have found a father-substitute of sorts in Eugen Bleuler, his chief at Burghölzli. But when he became acquainted with the writings of Freud in 1906, he was so inspired by their content and the force of expression that he initiated an exchange of letters with Freud, and eventually adopted him as a new father figure in place of Bleuler. After some correspondence, the two men had their first meeting in Vienna in 1907. Jung was invited to visit with him in February, and Jung says of that first encounter, "We met a one o'clock in the afternoon and talked virtually without a pause for thirteen hours."[12] Jung said that Freud was the first man of importance that he had ever met up until that point in his life, and he found him to be extremely intelligent and not in the least trivial.

This initial encounter took place on March 3, 1907 (**exactly when the AP was making a square with the Lunar Nodes**). The

---

[11]H.F. Ellenberger, *The Discovery of the Unconscious*, Basic Books, NY, 1970.
[12]See *Memories, Dreams, Reflections*, p. 149. The reader should really investigate the complete chapter, pp. 146-169.

aspects suggest that the meeting would have far-reaching results for both men (or for Jung at least). The fact that squares were involved is an indication of the tension and dynamism that lay in the meeting and the subsequent relationship with Freud. These squares kept Jung busily engaged in the relationship for a long time.

Lunar Nodes in the second house demand fertility, the exploration of all possible avenues and the utilization of one's personal abilities and of all the powers accruing to one from within and without. That the meeting with Freud took place under a square aspect to the Moon's Nodes shows that Freud managed to throw Jung back on his own resources: through the method of dream analysis, Freud placed in his hands a means of understanding his first childhood dreams, which came to him along with other information from the "greater No. 2."

Contrary to the commonly held opinion, Jung differed from Freud in his theoretical ideas right from the start. Thus, even before their first meeting, Jung made statements to that effect. In a letter written to Freud on December 29, 1906, Jung mentions that he "understands" that Freud cannot be pleased with his book (*The Psychology of Dementia Praecox*) and discusses the fact that they do not see eye to eye. He writes that his material is totally different from Freud's, his working conditions are totally different, and here Jung states that he is working with uneducated insane people, implying that Freud is working with a different kind of patient. He also states that his background and environment are totally different, as well as mentioning that his experience is limited in comparison to Freud's. At the end of his dissertation about why they are so different, Jung is deferential by saying that Freud must have more talent than he, and that he, Jung, was bereft of having a chance to study with Freud himself, and therefore his training was, as Jung puts it, "regrettably defective."[13]

The significant fact, that from the outset Jung did not go along with Freud in all his views (thus sowing the seeds of their future discord and separation), is overlooked by many. Freud found in Jung not some poor parrot of a pupil, but someone with whom he could confer, someone with a mind of the same caliber as his own. It was precisely the spontaneously occurring polarity between the two

---

[13]*The Freud/Jung Letters*, edited by William McGuire, translated by Ralph Manheim and R.F.C. Hull, Bollingen Series, XCIV, Princeton University Press, Princeton, NJ, 1976, p. 14.

men in regard to their different religious (!) views that set in motion a dynamic interaction out of which the psychoanalytical movement eventually sprang. I venture to suggest that their differences arose from their religious opinions, because I regard sexuality mainly as a religious and not a scientific phenomenon (which certainly does not prevent us from approaching the subject from the scientific angle, as has been done for hundreds of years to a noteworthy degree by the tantric Yogis and Buddhists of India and Tibet, and by the Taoist sages of China, all of whom have left us writings and teaching which are full of wisdom).

The conjunction of the AP with Mercury (**September, 1907**) seems to be double-edged in its effect: 1) Officially Jung presented himself at the International Congress for Psychiatry and Neurology as a spokesman for Freud in the heated discussion about hysteria (September, 1907), and two months later he read a report on psychoanalysis to the Zurich Medical Association. It is to be remembered that, at this time, psychoanalysis with its daring new theories was a highly controversial subject, and all those who advocated these theories were lumped together (just as astrologers are today). 2) In spite of his official sponsorship of Freud, Jung was already expressing profound doubts. In a letter dated August 19, 1907, Jung asks a number of veiled questions regarding Freud's concept of sexuality.[14]

Jung vacillated between doubt and conviction during that time—which is typical of the versatile, analytical nature of Mercury. That eroticism and sexuality dominated his thought processes is clearly defined by the presence of Venus (conjunct Mercury).

● Age Point Moving from LP of the 6th House to Cusp 7 (Age 33-36)

Life crisis

With the transit of the AP over Venus and over LP 6 (**July, 1908**), various interesting events occur. Venus in Cancer understandably gives a wish for a house of one's own and the position at

---

[14]For further details, see *The Freud/Jung Letters*, p. 79.

the LP points to withdrawal and settling down in a private sphere; hence it is not surprising that Jung had a house of his own design built for himself at the lower end of the Lake of Zurich.

One year later (**April, 1909**), two months after the **exact Low Point 6**, he resigned his position at the Burghölzli in order to go into private practice as a psychotherapist in Küsnacht. At this time (July, 1909) there was also a quincunx to Mars, which has a highly sensitive placement in Sagittarius, indicating rich erotic urges, but in the eleventh house these were held tightly in check by his puritanical upbringing and morality (his father was a clergyman!).

And so a phase began in the shadow of the next house with its doubts, anxieties and motives for changes of direction—and Jung entered that stage of practical psychological experience through which every budding analyst and therapist must pass, even today, if he is not to remain one of those cerebral theorists we all too often encounter. In a letter Jung wrote to Freud on March 7, 1909, he recounts such an illuminating experience, for he discusses a problem that is often confronted by serious therapists. Evidently an old patient that he once treated created a scandal because Jung denied himself the pleasure of making her pregnant. He was very hurt because his intentions were honorable, he was a gentleman with the lady, and because of the doctor/patient relationship, he was forced to look at an old complex. He says, "Meanwhile I have learnt an unspeakable amount of marital wisdom, for until now I had a totally inadequate idea of my polygamous components despite all self-analysis."[15]

In the same year, 1909, when he was thirty-four, Jung made the acquaintance of a female patient, Miss T. Wolff, who was to play an important part in his later life. T. Wolff was a shy and reserved young woman of twenty-one who had recently lost her father.

In the beginning, Jung was fully aware of the complexes that gripped him so strongly, although the sensitive Venus in Cancer at the Low Point, over which the AP was moving, shows that he must have been experiencing a powerful life crisis (**LP 6**) aggravated by an erotic crisis (Venus). His polygamous components surfaced in subsequent years to the extent that T. Wolff was increasingly accepted into Jung's family and became his semi-official mistress.

---

[15]Readers may wish to read this letter. See *The Freud/Jung Letters*, p. 207.

It is specifically in this sector (**stretching from LP 6 to cusp 7**) that Jung was compelled to accept, assimilate and integrate an irruption into his world of personal relationships, and this led to a temporary diffusion of his concepts of existence.

Obviously, a second relationship like the one with T. Wolff would entail, in years to come, a conscious confrontation in partnership matters (**passage of the Age Point to the DC**). This point represents the opposite number, and the transits to the seventh house, which have always been associated with relationships with the partner in marriage and work.

• Age Point in the 7th House
   (Age 36-42)

The break with Freud

In **February 1912** the AP transited the Sun and then the problem of the father relationship came to a head and demanded a solution, especially as the square between the Sun and Neptune entered in as a disturbing factor.

That Freud, Jung's senior by nineteen years, was elevated to the rank of father-figure seemed only fair to the latter and Freud encouraged this state of affairs to the extent that he called Jung his "crown prince" who one day would spread psychoanalysis still further when Freud was dead and gone. Others regarded this as a very privileged position and many might have striven hard to attain it. No so Jung.

Jung's psyche, which was seeking wholeness, simply had to integrate the father-figure projected on Freud. For this purpose, the father-figure had first to be detached from the object, *i.e.*, from Freud; in other words, the relationship with Freud had to be severed. Admittedly, the very patriarchally inclined Sigmund Freud helped to promote this process of detachment by demanding "absolute obedience and toeing of the psychoanalytical party line," which incited the rebellious Leo Sun in Jung, with its craving for freedom from restraint, to thrust him still further from Freud's side. And anyway, Freud broke with other disciples who would not kowtow to him (first of all A. Adler). Therefore it was not so much the differences in their psychological theories, as the realities of personal development and egotism, that precipitated the break between these two pioneers of the psyche.

In astro-psychology the Sun stands for the principle of self-consciousness. With the transit of the AP over the Sun an individual can and must be himself; the will to engage in independent thought and action is strengthened, as we see in letters written by Jung to Freud.

Six months after the transit of the Sun by the AP, Jung wrote (on December 18, 1912) to question Freud's behavior with his students. The letter is basically an attack, for Jung says that he is being straightforward and ambivalent now that he has discovered a particular behavior pattern of Freud's. It seems that Freud surrounded himself with psychoanalysts and in meetings with them brought out certain weaknesses that he then used to keep everyone in their place. Jung stated that this behavior would only produce "slavish sons or puppies" and not good thinkers. He questioned Freud's behavior, saying, "For sheer obsequiousness nobody dares to pluck the prophet by the beard and inquire for once what you would say to a patient with a tendency to analyse the analyst instead of himself. You would certainly ask him: *'Who's* got the neurosis?'"[16]

This was only one of a whole series of "confidential letters" showered upon Freud. For the partriarchally-minded founder of psychoanalysis, this pugnacious letter was a shot that slipped through his guard (Jung had Mars in Sagittarius, the Archer!) and it left Freud no option but to climb down from the seat of authority to meet his colleagues unconditionally on equal terms, or to purge the psychoanalytical movement of such rash and mulish spirits.

To my mind, this demand for partnership is an essential expression of Jung's Age Point progression through the seventh house, which is also the house where his Sun is posited. Therefore, we are looking here at a central problem in Jung's life. It is plain to see in the letter discussed above how partnerships are regarded by the Leo Sun, which would rather rule than serve: "You and I are equal partners, and I am telling you how our relationship must develop," says Leo.

Six months later (**July, 1913**) there is a trine to the Moon's Node, that is to say, another aspect to the Lunar Node under which the relationship between the two men had begun: the relationship

---

[16]*The Freud Jung Letters*, pp. 534-35.

was commenced under the square aspect, and was dissolved under the trine.

So much for the traditional teaching that the trine is "good" and the square is "bad." The square showed strength and initiative and promoted active behavior, while the trine to the Lunar Node represented the first step toward self-realization. In this it was possible for Jung to break free and extricate himself from the involvement with that external object, the projected father figure.

Another way of looking at it is this: under the square aspect Jung was fated to attend to unfinished business; he used the unresolved father problem as a dynamic component. The transit of the Sun activated his complex and the approaching trine to the Moon's Node enabled him to explore for himself, and to profit by, the rich experiences of the previous few years. This he had to do on his own without some father-figure breathing down his neck. The break with Freud was therefore unavoidable, and what occasioned it was not so much their differences of opinion as the striving of Jung's psyche after integration and self-development.

● LP of 7th House to Virgo

The interim period

This digging into his resources turned out to be much more difficult than Jung had anticipated. After his break with Freud, he made a veritable journey into the underworld, which H. F. Ellenberger has called the "interim period," or even the "creative illness."[17] As the AP entered the area of consciousness (above the horizon in the horoscope), Jung commenced a self-analysis of the images and phantasies that gushed from his unconscious with ever increasing force. That these images were also warnings of collective events, namely an anticipation of the happenings of World War I, did not become clear to him until very much later. Since his self-analysis provides the key to Jung's whole system of psychology, we shall share one of his dreams with you. Note that during this period the **IP was in the 7th house**, and the **AP would move to a conjunction with Uranus in January 1914.**

---

[17]H.F. Ellenberger, *The Discovery of the Unconscious*, Basic Books, NY, 1970.

During this period one of his profound dreams involved a sinking to the depths. Jung had a vision on December 12, 1913, as he was sitting meditatively thinking about his fears. He let himself drop and found himself plunging into dark depths. He could not fend off a feeling of panic, but that was soon averted as he landed in some sort of a sticky mass. His eyes became accustomed to the gloom of the darkness and he was able to make out the entrance to a cave. Inside the cave stood a dwarf, which Jung describes as looking mummified for his skin was very leathery. He squeezed past this dwarf and got inside, wading knee deep through icy water to the other end of the cave. There he sees a glowing red crystal, and he grabbed the stone, finding a hollow underneath. Then he saw running water. The water must have changed in depth, for it carried a corpse—a youth with blond hair with a headwound, followed by a black scarab, followed by a red and newborn sun that rose out of the depths of the water. He was overcome by the light and wanted to replace the stone upon the opening in the cave, but he found that when he did this, some kind of a fluid welled out. Looking closer, he saw that the fluid was blood, and he became nauseated. The blood seemed to keep coming out for a very long time. Finally it stopped, and his vision was over.[18]

This dream occurred six months after the trine to the Lunar Node, almost exactly when the AP was conjunct Uranus. What is more, Uranus itself was transiting in the vicinity of the Ascendant at this time, and was moving between 3-7° Aquarius.

When we leave Uranus behind there is a considerable stretch in the chart before we come to Jupiter. Jung's "descent to Avernus" can also be seen as the long journey through the empty space. The inner significance of an empty phase like this is, generally speaking, to cultivate and harvest the fruit of the soil broken up by previous transits of planets.

Now one of the things Uranus is good at helping us to do is building bridges into infinity, in order to leave behind the known, and to press forward into the untried. Metaphorically, Jung slithered into the depths down the radical trine between Uranus and the Lunar Node, and down the square to the Moon into the great Deep, where he encountered the brute force of the archetypal images and made his way across the great trapezium and up to the holistic realm of Jupiter.

---

[18]See *Memories, Dreams, Reflections,* p. 179.

In addition (**February, 1914**), the square of the AP to the Moon churned up his emotions, and these were investigated and interpreted with Uranian scholarly ardor. Jung made forceful reference to this process in *Memories, Dreams, Reflections*, where he discusses releasing an incessant stream of fantasies, and that he had difficulty trying to understand what was happening to him. In this work he states clearly that he felt helpless, the world felt alien to him, everything seemed hard to understand. He lived in a constant state of tension. He felt a strength that was close to demonic when he needed to find the meaning in his experiences and he endured the assaults of the unconscious because he was also convinced that he was obeying a higher will. This feeling helped give him the endurance he needed to follow through. By continuing with the imagery, he was able to actually find the images that were concealed in the emotions, and when he could do that, he felt more calm and reassured. He talks about the challenge—he could have left the images hidden in the emotions, but felt that he might be torn to pieces by their very existence—or he could succeed in splitting them off and then would have developed neuroses that would have destroyed him anyway. By experiencing this encounter with the unconscious images in a personal way, he learned how valuable it was to find the images that lie behind the emotions. While pursuing this stage of his life, Jung speaks of his commitment to the future of his patients, for by knowing that he would someday be able to help others, he was able to endure the pain of his own experience.[19] This is typical of Jung's Moon placement: in the radix, the Moon as the emotional self is flanked on each side by the so-called spiritual planets Pluto and Neptune, and these lend their support to the Moon as the "purest of motives," as selfless impulses and as suprapersonal goals.

● Age Point at Cusp 8 and in the 8th House (Age 42-48)

Process of transformation

Jung's journey through the unconscious continued until about 1919, and with the entry of the AP into Virgo (**July 1916**) a change began to make itself felt. In *Memories, Dreams, Reflections*, he

---

[19]See *Memories, Dreams, Reflections*, pp. 176-79.

discusses the fact that an inner change was taking place within him. He felt (1916) an urge to give shape to something, literally compelled from within. The work was pushed through in the midst of some parapsychological phenomena, and was named *Septem Sermones ad Mortuos*, a privately printed work subtitled "The Seven Sermons of the Dead written by Basilides in Alexandria, the city where the East toucheth the West."[20]

The torrent of phantasies abated, and as the AP passed through the shadow of the eighth house cusp, he began analyzing and organizing the imagery that had emerged. The unconscious pushed him to face the death-and-becoming processes of the eighth house, and has to be seen as one of the most difficult stages in the journey of life. A rather aggressive period following the transit of the seventh cusp and the radical Sun had now given way to inner seeking and to inner renewal.

In December 1916 (that is to say just before the exit from the shadow of the eighth cusp), Jung delivered a lecture in Paris on "La structure de l'inconscient" (The structure of the unconscious), out of which developed his extremely important and foundational work, *Two Essays on Analytical Psychology*, which was published twelve years later (when the MC was transited). In this lecture and the subsequent elucidations, he expounded his own concepts of the unconscious, and commenced to develop his ideas about the collective unconscious and about the stages in the individuation process (persona, shadow, animus/anima, the self or mana-personality). With this step into the eighth house (in which, as we know, there is a recognition of structures and their changes), the step beyond Freud was fully taken. With the concept of a collective region of the psyche, that is to say of a region of the psyche common to the human race, he laid the foundation stone of an edifice to house his ideas on the transpersonal—an action very much in keeping with the character of the eighth house.

AP halfway between two figures

In Age Point research, a regularity has been discovered which is plainly perceptible in Jung's chart. If the AP leaves one aspect figure and travels through empty space, a kind of switch over from old to

---

[20]See *Memories, Dreams, Reflections*, pp. 189-91.

new takes place halfway between two figures. In Jung's case the halfway mark is circa 19° Virgo. This corresponds to **April, 1919.**

Now Jung describes how two events signaled the end of his journey through the unconscious: in the winter of 1918/19 (in October, 1918, the AP made a trine to the Moon and in January, 1919, a sextile to Venus) he severed his connection with a lady who tried to persuade him that the pictures in which he painted his phantasies from the unconscious possessed artistic merit and wanted to sell them. Secondly, he began to draw mandalas which, so to speak, as "cryptograms of his Self," indicated his growth into wholeness.

● Age Point at Cusp 8 (Age 45)

In 1921 he published, in German, the book *Psychological Types*,[21] in which he presented a new way of looking at depth psychology. It was his first major work since separating from Freud. The Age Point was making a sextile with the Sun in March 1921, and this suggests a degree of public success. Soon afterwards, in April 1921, the AP made contact with the LP of the eighth house, a significant point for psychological change in the sense of death-and-becoming: something old, on which he had worked hard until it finally materialized in this book, was completed, and something new, which was already present in the germ, could and indeed should begin to grow.

It is an interesting fact that the book on psychological types is still relatively unknown even today and its statements on the psychology of the conscious mind are for the most part neglected. Presumably this is because the Age Point was transiting the Low Point of the eighth house. This point ushers in a time when the native turns inwards, winds up an old course of action and manages to change direction.

Psychological Types represents the breakthrough into the outer world after his tour of some eight years through the "underworld."

---

[21]C.G. Jung, *Psychological Types*, published in English by Harcourt, Brace & Jovanovich in the U.S.A., and by Routledge & Kegan Paul in the U.K.

In the next few years the Age Point in Jung's chart drew nearer and nearer to the other great trapezoid figure and the No. 2 personality began to coalesce with the No. 1 personality. The father-figure was integrated into the self as the trapezium unfolded its whole wealth of potential.

● Age Point in the 9th House (Age 48-54)

Travels, expansion of consciousness, energetics

With the entry of the Age Point into Libra (September 1920) there were several trips to Tunis and Algiers. Now here is a typical case in which the planet Jupiter and the cusp of the 9th house (both of them having to do with journeys and both in Libra) start to exert a powerful action as soon as there is a change of sign. Further information on the significance of changes of sign will be found in Chapter 2 of Part I.

In **December, 1923** the AP/Jupiter conjunction was exact. Shortly afterwards he visited the Pueblo Indians in Arizona and Mexico (1924/25).

The year 1928 was another fateful year. The AP reached the **opposition to Pluto in October of that year**, and this had already brought about a radical change when it conjuncted in 1892. Pluto symbolizes the higher self and its powers of metamorphosis and, with the opposition to this planet, Jung placed a paper before the public which indicated his contemporary views ("On Psychic Energy," 1928).

Jung felt a great need to understand the libido, for he conceived it as a psychic analogue of physical energy. He felt that it should be judged in quantitative and not qualitative terms, for he wanted to escape from the then prevalent concretism of the theory. He did not wish to speak of the libido as an instinct of hunger or aggression or sex, but rather wanted to regard all of these instincts as a form of psychic energy. If libido was considered as an energy form, an actual understanding of libido would allow the observer to let sexuality, power, or hunder recede into the background, while allowing the libido to be observed in a more scientific view. His paper, "On Psychic Energy," was an attempt to express this idea.[22]

---

[22]See *Memories, Dreams, Reflections*, pp. 208-09.

Another event occurred to help Jung along. Richard Wilhelm sent him the manuscript of a Chinese treatise, *The Secret of the Golden Flower*, and through this manuscript he came in contact with alchemy and oriental mysticism which held a powerful attraction for him from that time forward. The spiritual penetration of alchemy and its reinterpretation from a psychological point of view is probably one of Jung's greatest and most gratifying gifts to posterity. He rescued this important empirical material produced by generations of seekers for the "stone of the wise" from the musty past. Quite incidentally he founded a new method of unlocking both individual psychic contents and old texts through the technique of amplification.[23]

• Age Point in the 10th and 11th Houses (Age 54-66)

Success, recognition and peak of activity

In July, 1929, in collaboration with Richard Wilhelm, he issued the book, *The Secret of the Golden Flower*,[24] at a time when he, himself, was in the flower of life. As he wrote in retrospect that after he reached the central point of his thinking and understood the basic concept of the *self*, he was able to go back to the world. He lectured and travelled a great deal. The lectures and writing formed a counterpoise for the years commited to the search within. They also contained questions and answers that were brought up by both readers and patients.[25]

---

[23]While it is true that Jung introduced the subject of alchemy to the psychological fraternity, and while it is also true that several of his books reproduce many valuable alchemical illustrations (some of which it would be hard for the general reader to find elsewhere), we should not imagine that he salvaged the material single-handedly. A renewed interest was being shown in the old works before Jung came on the scene, and a number of them had been republished. Indeed, he can be accused of distorting their meaning quite unscientifically, by lacing them with the jargon of twentieth century psychology instead of coming to terms with the thought of the various periods in which they were written. *Tr.*

[24]*The Secret of the Golden Flower*, translated by Richard Wilhelm, with a foreword and commentary by C.G. Jung. First published in England by Routledge and Kegan Paul, London, 1931.

[25]C.G. Jung, *Memories, Dreams, Reflections*, p. 208.

The transit of the tenth and eleventh houses thrust Jung into the public eye. He found recognition of his work and was honored an an eminent specialist in the psychological sphere. It is amazing how well his life at this time fits with the tenth house theme. Readers should also note that he put in a great deal of work in the earlier years, and the work bore fruit at this time.

● Age Point in the 12th House (Age 66-72)

Myocardial infarction and other diseases

We are now making a leap forward into the twelfth house. LP 12 occurs in November of 1943, and the next important stage of Jung's life is in complete accord with the dicta of classical astrology: in December of 1943 the AP made a quincunx to Uranus in Leo, which traditionally indicates problems with the heart. And in fact, at the beginning of 1944 Jung suffered from a serious myocardial infarction (after breaking a joint) and began to see visions. As life approached its limits, he saw himself flying away from the earth and had the same sight of our terrestrial globe as that enjoyed by a modern astronaut. Nowadays we would classify these visions as a genuine trans-personal peak-experience. Since A. Maslow made them accessible to psychological research we know how trans-forming such experiences can be.

The impact made by this imagery must have some connection with the **trine to the Moon** that occurred in **February 1944**. The visions persisted for three weeks, until Jung was off the danger list.

It was not until half a year later (July 1944, to be precise), that Jung resumed active correspondence (**AP in opposition to Venus**). Therefore, the period between Invert Point and Low Point in the twelfth house was a time of inner separation from the world. This is characteristically a time when many people give up and begin to withdraw from life.

In the shadow of the Ascendant, in November of 1946, Jung suffered another coronary embolism, and was once more confined to bed. The exact timing of this embolism, like that of the infarction at the beginning of 1944, is not shown in the Age Progression. This can sometimes be predicted by progression, but not necessarily always. The cause of disease lies deep below the surface and can sometimes be avoided, or it may rise earlier in life, and not be taken care of.

Thanks to his indomitable Leo nature, Jung recovered from this setback, too, and a month later he wrote to his friend Father V. White to share how he felt. It is really moving to read a letter in which Jung states that the *aspectus mortis* is a lonely thing, for "one is stripped of everything in the presence of God." He tells of a dream that he had, where he saw a bluish diamond-like star in heaven, and it was reflected in a pool—heaven above, heaven below. He related himself to the *imago Dei* in the darkness of the earth, and said that the dream was a great personal consolation. He mentions that he is ready to die, but there are still powerful thoughts coming to him— not his, but belonging to God. And at this phase of his life he feels that everything worth mentioning really belongs to God, or the universe.[26]

This description of Jung's experience when he was having a close encounter with death bears witness to the marvelous things that can happen to people when they enter the shadow of the AC. He had gained access to his true self, to his source, and, with the transit of the AC, underwent a new beginning, until the transit of Saturn brought a return of the illness.

● Age Point in the 1st House (Age 72-78)

Answer to Job

In the early summer of 1951 Jung suffered from a disease of the liver. On this occasion he concerned himself not with death but with the pressing problem of God and of the true content of religion, which has already been broached in his letter. Although he strove to preserve a scientific and empirical point of view, one cannot help noticing that he abandoned this and trespassed on the preserves of the theologians. This was taken very much amiss by many, and he was subjected to a great deal of criticism (conjunction with Saturn).

---

[26]*Selected Letters of C.G. Jung, 1909-1961*, selected and edited by Gerhard Adler, in collaboration with Aniela Jaffee; translated from the German by R.F.C. Hull. First Princeton/Bollingen Paperback printing in 1984, pp. 69, 70.

It was a hard and lonely time full of mental wrestling over the true nature of man.

Once more (as in 1879 when he was very young) the transit of Saturn signalled uncertainty about his "home," but this time there was no external situation unsettling him through changes of residence, nor was he being bullied by a dominating mother-figure; he was worrying about his spiritual home, and about the form in which God may be experienced. The book that came out of his search for God, *Answer to Job*,[27] can be seen as one of Jung's most significant works.

A newly awakened inner motive force had taken hold of him after the transit to the AC. He said he had to overcome a great internal resistance before he could write *Answer to Job*. He felt that the external root of this work lay in his environment as many questions from public as well as patients obliged him to express himself more clearly over the religious problems of modern man. He hesitated for years because he was aware of the storm it would raise. But in the end he couldn't refrain from coming to grips with a problem so urgent. It never crossed his mind that anyone would think he was proclaiming a metaphysical truth, but the theologians did not understand his psychological thinking.[28] And Jung experienced again the restraints of Saturn as criticism and doubt, and had trouble taming his Leo nature.

● Age Point in the 2nd House (Age 78-84)

Memories, Dreams, Reflections

Early in 1953 (**February**), T. Wolff died very suddenly at the quincunx to the Sun, as Jung's AP was approaching the cusp of the second house. Then some two years later his wife, Emma, died (**November 27, 1955**) with the AP exactly at Invert Point 2 and sextile

---

[27]C.G. Jung, *Answer to Job*. First published in German as *Antwort auf Hiob*, Zurich, 1952; first published in England in 1954. Available in the U.S.A. in the Bollingen Series, *Psychology East and West*, Princeton University Press; in the U.K. by Routledge & Kegan Paul.
[28]See *Memories, Dreams, Reflections*, pp. 216-217.

Pluto. There now followed a time of loneliness and retirement, and the strength of his own integration was repeatedly tested. He wrote to Erich Neumann on December 15, 1955 (quincunx Jupiter, semisextile Saturn), that the shock he experienced was so great that he could not concentrate or recover the power of speech. He said that two days before his wife's death, he had what he called a great illumination which lit up an old secret that had been embodied in her, and which exerted a tremendous influence on his life. Her quick and painless end, plus the transformative experience, were of great comfort to him. But the stillness, the audible silence, the empty air and the infinite distance were hard for him to bear at this time.[29]

And yet, in this vacuum, Jung prepared his last great work, which many have regarded as the key to the Jungian world of ideas—his autobiographic *Memories, Dreams, Reflections.* People had often spoken to him about having a biography written, but he had consistently refused to entertain the idea until, in the spring of 1957, he finally overcame his reluctance just as the AP reached LP 2 (**April, 1957**).

It is interesting to note that the publication of *Psychological Types* is associated with the Low Point of the Eighth house, and this new and important work with the Low Point of the opposite house.

Aniela Jaffe, the editor of *Memories, Dreams, Reflections*— without whom it would certainly never have seen the light of day— recollects how it was to work with Jung on this volume. The book was begun in the spring of 1957, at the request of the publisher, Kurt Wolff, and it was to be done as an autobiography—in Jung's own words. She asked him questions and recorded Jung's replies. At first she reports that he was reticent, but he soon got involved in the work, talking about himself and his development. At the end of the year, she noted that Jung, himself, noted a connection between images of his childhood and works that he had written in his old age.[30] One can see here how the years of childhood represented by the first two houses (and the AP moving through them for the second time) are brought back afresh—to be regarded in a new light.

In **April, 1958** Jung ended the three chapters on childhood and school years. This date coincides with the conjunction of the Lunar Node, which had played such an important part in Jung's life.

---

[29]*Selected Letters of C.G. Jung, 1909-1961,* pp. 145-46.
[30]See *Memories, Dreams, Reflections,* p. xiii.

The following year, as the AP traversed the region between the Lunar Node and Neptune, Jung concentrated on letter writing and on finishing his "memoirs." He also wrote a contribution to *Man and His Symbols*, in which he strove to present his system of psychology as clearly and as simply as possible, since he realized that he was addressing the lay public to a much greater extent than he had previously supposed. The "memoirs" are free from the aggressiveness and impulsiveness of former years. They are a circumspect work full of inner life, in which Jung expresses one or two personal convictions, conscious of the "jester's license" granted to old age.

Ms. Jaffe describes the final phase of the book with additional insight, for as the book took shape, a certain transformation and objectivization also took place in Jung. He was able to see himself and the significance of his life in an impersonal way. He said that if he was asked the value of his life, he would only be able to measure himself against the centuries and that he would definitely say it meant something. But if his value was only measured by contemporary ideas, it would mean nothing.[31] This impersonality becomes obvious more and more as one continues to read the book.

On **June 6, 1961,** Jung died peacefully at the very time signified by the conjunction of the AP with Neptune, and escaped from this world in order to travel in another realm. He left behind many volumes containing the results of his investigations into the human psyche, and these were to have a fruitful influence on Western psychology for decades to come.

---

[31]See *Memories, Dreams, Reflections,* pp. v-viii.

Chapter 2

Example Horoscopes

● Introduction

In this next chapter, with the help of three more example charts, we shall be taking a look at the meaning of the Age Point as it traverses a limited sector. We shall choose one moment in the life and describe the situation found at that time. This will reveal the positions in a chart which one needs to consider in order to understand the life situation as a whole.

● Chart 1

Calculation of the Age Point

We shall first give a quick way of calculating the degree reached by the Age Point shown in figure 2.2.1 on page 207. If we allow six years per house, the Age Point will be in the ninth house when the native is fifty-one (because when he was 48 the AP crossed the ninth cusp). But to pin-point the house position of the AP on the native's fifty-first birthday we need to know the size of the house. By inspection, we find that there are 17°29′ in the ninth house in figure 2.2.1. We now need to work out how many degrees the AP moves in a year in a house of this size. There are two methods of doing this.

One is to divide the number of house degrees by six: 17°29′ : 6 = 2°54′50″. The other is to turn to the AP-LP-IP table in *Life Clock* Vol. 1, pp. 38-39.

Find 17 in the House Size column and run your
finger along to the Per Year column   2°50′

For the remaining 29′ take 30′ in the House Size
column for "minutes" and find the corresponding
Per Year value   0°05′

By addition, the annual Age Point progression is   2°55′

For three years (48 + 3 = 51) this comes to 3 × 2°55′   8°45′

These 8°45′ are now added to the position of the
ninth cusp in Capricorn   + 16°31′

                                                                           ─────────
                                                                            = 25°16′

And so, on the fifty-first birthday (November 18, 1973) the Age Point stands at about 25° Capricorn. The next step is to look in the radix for any planets in the region of 25°. The Sun is 25°32′ Scorpio and the Dragon's Head is 26°33′ Virgo. Since the AP moves very slowly in such a small house as this one, the permissable orb is 1°. In a larger house, it would be half a degree.

Therefore at this age there is an exact sextile to the Sun, and in a few months the AP makes a trine with the lunar node. Each AP aspect, however, must be seen and interpreted not in isolation but in relation to other aspects past and future. This is especially important when the AP is contacting, in quick succession, planets linked by aspect in the radix. In the present example, the sequence running up to the Sun began with the sextile to Mercury. This was followed by the square to Saturn (15°), the quincunx to Neptune (18°) and the sextiles to the Moon and Sun. Finally there was a trine to the lunar node, at which point the process more or less came to an end.

In figure 2.2.1, the Moon is conjunct the Sun (the new-moon position) in the sixth house, the house of coping with life. These are ego planets (the Sun representing self-awareness, the Moon a more

Figure 2.2.1. Chart 1 is a male born on November 18, 1922, at 17:00h in Teufen, Switzerland. At age 51 the Age Point will be in the ninth house at 25°16′ Capricorn.

emotional sense of self), and in the sixth house they manifest themselves mainly in the areas of profession, work and duty. When the AP aspects the Sun, the Moon is implicated, too, because of their conjunction. The native has a solar standpoint but, in the process of achieving relative independence in the ninth house, cannot entirely avoid childish modes of behavior or unconscious anxieties about life. These need to be dealt with by the conscious mind. Since the Age Point aspect was made from the ninth house, the native had to think for himself about striking a balance and about reaching a decision on whether he ought to be working just to earn a living and to get on in the world, or whether he ought to be striving for idealistic and less selfish goals.

Accordingly, the native decided to become heavily involved in community affairs, and although this absorbed much of his time and energy it gave him more satisfaction than anything he had ever done. He managed to overcome his sense of insecurity and occasional fear of failure (sixth house) and, by accepting public responsibilities, was able to mature and to become stronger both in self-awareness and in sense of self. His life and work took on a deeper significance. What helped to make this possible was that the sextile formed to the ego planets by the Age Point from the ninth house served to distance the native somewhat from his personal problems, and added a whole new dimension to his awareness. He himself created the conditions for self-improvement. The planets below the horizon became effective and he gained a better understanding of his self-consciousness in all its weaknesses and strengths. By making the right decision he was able to take an essential step in his further development.

● Chart 2

In figure 2.2.2 the Age Point is not posited at the beginning of a sign or on a house cusp, nor is there a planet near it, so we need to look at any aspects; in this case a trine to Pluto. In addition, everything we do with the current situation has to be carefully weighed. We must not miss the fact that the AP has recently made a sextile to Mars. We have also to check what is going to happen next, since this is often significant for the current situation. The Age Point is in Scorpio in the region of experience we call the eighth house. This is the predominant theme. Pluto is in Cancer and just approaching the fifth house. Mars and Venus are in opposition to Pluto, and these three planets work together as a functional unit; their individual qualities being stimulated one after the other by AP aspects. The color of the aspects is blue, so we may safely assume an absence of struggle at this stage and an effortless learning process arising from a harmonious experience of the properties of the three planets. There are no hard or awkward circumstances with which to deal. The influences of the 5/11 axis can be met and mastered with calm confidence. Since the native is not being pressured, he is much less likely to react ill-advisedly.

Figure 2.2.2. Chart 2 is a male born on January 19, 1930, at 10:30h in Baar, Switzerland. On his 44th birthday, the Age Point is 17°28′ Capricorn.

Age Point aspects are effective for about one degree on either side of the exact position, depending on the house size. All AP aspects to the house cusps, except transits, are found to be inoperative, but changes of sign are very powerful.

We must now define the successive positions of the AP. The theme of the third quadrant is the confrontation between the ego and its opposite number, between the external world and the individual who seeks his freedom. Half-way round this quadrant, in the fixed (*i.e.*, succedent) house, the native encounteres those structures that weld human beings into communities. The eighth house issue is joined not (as in the seventh) with separate persons, but with the organization of the community, with its laws, rules and conventions and, in a higher sense, with the laws of nature.

In these years (42-48) the emphasis is on the native's psychological reactions: he seeks comprehension, and wants to undergo a process of transformation. His emotional world is liable to suffer a certain amount of upheaval. Structures he has erected are broken; perhaps he himself pulls them down because they stand in the way of his further development. He may see them as a burdensome obligation and may try to release himself from them or else starts living a double life. A peculiar inconsistency evidences itself: on the one hand there is the desire for personal freedom and on the other hand there is the intention to profit by what has been achieved so far. He looks for an assured place in the social framework, and, from this vantage point strives for recognition and status. But in Scorpio his treatment of society is controversial; a new answer has to be found.

The Pluto/Mars opposition along the 5/11 relationship axis, when viewed in this light, reveals problems in human relationships. The eighth house, especially in combination with the sign Scorpio, raises certain doubts as to whether the commitments made in the seventh house or under external pressure (shown by the opposition) were truly desired. The blue trine and sextile aspects tend to encourage a harmonious balance between the inner need for personal freedom and the requirements imposed by society. There are a number of ways of offsetting one against the other.

With an opposition along the 5/11 axis there is always a chance that the native will get himself trapped in some confining relationship. But where there are blue aspects in the eighth house, any problem-relationships (whatever their origin) can be tackled afresh with better prospects of solving them. In the present instance, the problems are particularly pressing, since the Sun, Mercury, and Venus are all in the eleventh house. There is an earnest desire to find true friendship, the right group, the ideal society; the native seeks congenial company. This theme now occupies the center of the individual's attention.

In Pluto we recognize a strong super-ego function. Here is an imposing, very capable person (fifth house) with obvious patriarchal qualities which would be exercised in a thoroughly philanthropic (Cancer) manner. This leading tendency stands in stark contrast to the eroticism signified by Mars and Venus. The latter planets make for idealism whereas Pluto makes for realism—and there is a constant conflict between the two. There is a powerful tension between the two poles, not only because they are in opposition but also because of their house position. Mars and Venus would have been better placed in the fifth house, and Pluto ought, for preference, to have occupied the cusp of the eleventh. Neither Mars/Venus nor Pluto can develop as they should, even with blue aspects in the eighth house. To know this may not be comforting but, like all true insights it has a liberating effect, is beneficial, and promotes a more balanced outlook. Indeed, the tension can be sublimated in creative work given the right motivation. That was what happened here—the native liked helping people and never stopped learning. As a lay medical practitioner he was always looking for new ways to solve physical problems, methods he could put to immediate use for the benefit of his patients.

As long as the Age Point was moving through the relatively empty space of the eighth and ninth houses, nothing much happened in his life. It was not until the LP of the ninth house and the run-up to the MC that the professional body to which he belonged approached him and asked for his active participation in various projects. And only at the MC (cusp of the tenth house) did he start to play a leading role, working since then in his official capacity just as progressively as he used to do in his small practice. To sum up, the aspect configuration centered on the planets at the top of the horoscope is very suitable for someone who takes a lead; especially in this case, where Saturn promises a sense of responsibility and Mars gives the necessary energy.

● Chart 3

Figure 2.2.3 on page 212 shows a momentous transit: the crossing from a ruling into a serving situation. The difference between the two signs is seen in a marked change in the attitude to life. In our example it is more marked than usual because Saturn on house cusp ten points clearly either to a ruling position or to the Leo wish to domineer. Shortly after the MC and Saturn are transited, the Age Point enters a serving sign—while still in the tenth house.

The owner of the hororscope in figure 2.2.3 was a dominant female, a matriarch who knew how to make herself obeyed. Her Virgo demands greater concern for humanity. The native takes an increasing interest in need and suffering; it is no longer possible to ignore them. The desired power must be renounced—or it will be taken away. The aspect configuration that indicates her ability to govern includes all three main planets. Her influence spreads itself over the thoughts and emotions of anyone under her physical control. The Sun is particularly well placed just inside the ninth cusp, and is very strong by sign. Saturn and Venus, the two classical female planets, are not far away. However, there is a small gap between them separating the two configurations to which they belong. The transition of the Age Point from one aspect configuration to the other signifies abandonment of the mothering role to return to pure femininity, Venus being female charm, and Saturn wifely care. The role-playing represented by Saturn is certainly much to the fore in the present case, because Saturn is on the MC in

Figure 2.2.3. Chart 3 is a female born July 23, 1919, at 15:00h in Langenthal, Switzerland. The Age Point is crossing from Leo to Virgo at age 55.

Leo, the sign in which role-playing is an aid to increased self-awareness. (Incidentally, the maternal function as an archetypal role is not limited to any given sex or age. It can also be assumed by men.) But at the transition point the maternal role is left behind and femininity *per se* comes to the fore together with a genuine helping function (Venus in Virgo). In Virgo this can mean a sympathetic response to the poor, the suffering and the weak—it can mean what we think of as "the woman's touch." The form taken by this response will depend on the situation and its possibilities, and on those around, but invariably there will be the desire to help or heal. The opposing Uranus points to welfare work and (assisted by the lunar node) could inaugurate changes when aspected. This could work out in such a way that opportunities for dedicated social service will offer themselves. After the change of sign, Uranus, the dragon's head, Mars, Venus and Pluto are all aspected in quick succession. Hence we have a veritable transformation or meta-morphosis (Pluto on cusp 9 producing a change in outlook) and a renewal of the personality from the mind outwards.

In the tenth house, this lady experienced a thorough reshaping of her life. Opportunities suddenly arose for using to the full her gifts for healing and relief work. She was highly successful in combining advisory and medical activities. Many people were able to thank her for helping them when they were in distress and she became a popular figure both inside and outside her own country.

Appendix

Age Point Calculation

Written by Michael A. Huber
Translated and edited by Michael P. Munkasey

Quick calculation explanation—Age Point movement and calculation—Mathematical calculation techniques—Time calculation in the houses—Examples using timing questions—Examples using zodiacal questions

● The Age Point Method and the Horoscope

The horoscope acts like a clock in one sense, and it is through the use of the horoscope as a clock that the position of the Age Point (AP) can be measured. The process of measuring the AP through the houses of the horoscope is called Age Progression. The speed of the AP through the horoscope can be compared to the speed of a car which a person is deliberately driving along a road. The road is like the zodiac, and the number of miles along the road that the driver moves can be compared to the distance in degrees of the zodiac that the AP advances as life continues. Just as the speed of the car along the highway is not always the same, the speed of the AP also varies as life's circumstances (*i.e.*, house sizes) change.

The speed of the AP changes every 6 years, as a new house is entered. The size of the house (the number of degrees that the house occupies) determines the speed, in degrees, that the AP progresses. The larger the house the greater the speed of the AP in degrees. The smaller the house the smaller the speed of the AP in degrees. The speed of the AP is constant through any one house, but the speed changes abruptly at the Koch house cusp. This change occurs every six years as the AP passes through each of the twelve houses of the horoscope.

As the AP passes through the house it makes contact with the planets and the Nodes in the house that it's in, as well as making aspects to the other planets and points in the horoscope. The AP will also encounter sign changes. As each of these aspects or contacts are made, the person will experience certain events in the real world which will be related to the nature of the horoscope event that has just occurred.

Here are the important things to remember about calculating the Age Point (AP) as it moves through the horoscope:

1. The AP passes through each house in six years, regardless of the size of the house.

2. Only the Koch House System is used with the Age Progression method.

3. The size of each house, in degrees and minutes, must be measured accurately.

4. The speed of the AP as it moves through each house is expressed in time units (*e.g.*, years, months, days, etc.). Therefore, to calculate the important times of life as determined by the AP, degree distances within the house must be converted to time units using the methods described later within this appendix.

Considerations

Because each house represents six years of life, the following numbers can be used as constants for all of the following AP calculations:

- One solar year = 365.25 days
- 72 solar years = One Horoscope cycle = 26,298.0 days
- One House = 6 Years = 2,191.5 days
- The Low Point of a House is reached 1,354 days after entering a house.

● The Invert Point of a House is reached 837.5 days after entering a house.

You may find that using a pocket calculator will be helpful for the following calculations. A small calculator that can add or subtract hours or minutes directly is the best type to use. However, any small calculator can be used to do these calculations. To find the daily speed of the AP through a house, perform calculations like these in the following examples:

1. Measure each house size, Koch cusp to Koch cusp, in degrees and minutes. For instance, if the Koch cusp of the 4th house is 20°00' Libra, and the Koch cusp of the 5th house is 10°05' Sagittarius, then the number of degrees in the 4th house is the number of degrees from 20 LIB 00 to 10 SAG 05. To measure this distance in degrees we measure from 20 LIB 00 to zero degrees of Scorpio, then measure 30 degrees for the sign of Scorpio (because Scorpio is intercepted in the 4th house), and then finally add the remaining 10 degrees and 05 minutes of Sagittarius that are left. Doing this we get:

Distance from 20 LIB 00 to 00 SCO 00	=		10°00'
Interception for the Sign of Scorpio	=		30°00'
Distance to 10 SAG 05	=	+	10°05'
4th House Size	=		50°05'

Similarly the size of the 2nd house, which goes from 1 VIR 18 on the 2nd house cusp to 25 VIR 37 on the 3rd house cusp is found by:

3rd House Cusp placement is 25 VIR 37	=		25°37'
2nd House Cusp placement is 1 VIR 18	=	-	1°18'
Subtracting one value from the other	=		24°19'

Therefore the 2nd house size is 24°19', while the 4th house size is 50°05'. Each of these degree distances will be travelled by the AP in exactly six years, or 2,191.5 days.

Take the following horoscope as an example:

Date of Birth = May 10, 1942
Time = 11:30 AM; Location = Zurich, Switzerland.

(This Chart) Location		Koch Cusps	(For all charts) Age (Years)	Age (Days)
1st House Cusp (AC)	=	7 LEO 06	0	0
2nd House Cusp	=	1 VIR 18	6	2191.5
3rd House Cusp	=	25 VIR 37	12	4383.0
4th House Cusp	=	20 LIB 00	18	6574.5
5th House Cusp	=	10 SAG 05	24	8766.0
6th House Cusp	=	11 CAP 37	30	10957.5
7th House Cusp	=	7 AQU 06	36	13149.0
8th House Cusp	=	1 PSC 18	42	15340.5
9th House Cusp	=	25 PSC 37	48	17532.0
10th House Cusp	=	20 ARI 00	54	19723.5
11th House Cusp	=	10 GEM 05	60	21915.0
12th House Cusp	=	11 CAN 37	66	24106.5
1st House Cusp	=	7 LEO 06	72	26298.0

VENUS at 4 ARI 41 in the 9th house

Notice that the zodiacal sign of Scorpio is intercepted in the 4th house, and that the zodiacal sign of Taurus is intercepted in the 10th house.

• Calculation of the Year Point

A "year point" is the location of the AP on a person's birthday. Each house gives six birthdays or year points. Each of the birthdates can be measured as an exact number of days from each house cusp, because the number of days in a year and in each house always remains the same. It is the speed of the AP that changes through each of the houses. Each year consists of 365.25 days. The first calculation we can then perform, once the house sizes (in degrees) are calculated, is to find out where the year points are in each house. Each house will have six year points within in. For example, the 3rd house will have the year points: 12 (at the cusp), 13, 14, 15, 16, and 17. The zodiacal position of the AP for each of these year points can be calculated once the size of the house is known. To calculate the size of the 3rd house, proceed as before:

Distance from 25 VIR 37 to 00 LIB 00	=	4°23′
Distance to 20 LIB 00	=	20°00′
3rd House Size	=	24°23′

Each of the year points will occur at a distance of 1/6 of the house size from the house cusp. In this example for the 3rd house, each year point will be alloted 1/6 of the 24°23′, or:

$$24°23′ \div 6 = 4°03′50″ \text{ or } 4°04′ \text{ approximately}$$

Using Table 1 on page 220 these calculations can be performed and broken down into different parts, as follows:

$$23′ = 0.38333333° \text{ (From Table 1)}$$
$$24° + 23′ = 24° + 0.38333333 = 24.38333333°$$
$$24.38333333° \div 6 = 4.06388888°$$
$$4.06388888° = 4° + 03′ + 50″ = 4°03′50″$$

The calculations to determine the year point intervals in degrees could have also been performed using a hand calculator in the following manner:

$$24° + (23 \div 60)° = 24.38333333°$$

(The degree part and the fractional minute part are added.)

$$24.38333333° \div 6 = 4.06388888°$$

(The sum is divided by the 6 years.)

This is equal to 4° plus 0.06388888°

(Taking the fractional part of this number)

$$0.063888888° \times 60 \text{ minutes} \div \text{degree} = 3.833328′$$

(The number to the left of the decimal point in this answer gives the MINUTES part.)

Subtracting the "3" part out, gives 3' as the MINUTES answer, and, leaves

0.833328 as the fractional part; multiplying this fractional part by 60 (seconds ÷ minute) again we get

49.99997 which is close enough to 50 when rounded off.

(This number is the SECONDS answer.)

Therefore, the answer (using a hand calculator) is the accumulation of all of these parts, or: 4°03'50" (which, rounded, is: 4° 04').

Table 1. Equivalences

Minute and Degree Equivalences		
1' = 0.0166666°	21' = 0.3500000°	41' = 0.68333333°
2' = 0.0333333°	22' = 0.3666666°	42' = 0.70000000°
3' = 0.0500000°	23' = 0.3833333°	43' = 0.71666666°
4' = 0.0666666°	24' = 0.4000000°	44' = 0.73333333°
5' = 0.0833333°	25' = 0.4166666°	45' = 0.75000000°
6' = 0.1000000°	26' = 0.4333333°	46' = 0.76666666°
7' = 0.1166666°	27' = 0.4500000°	47' = 0.78333333°
8' = 0.1333333°	28' = 0.4666666°	48' = 0.80000000°
9' = 0.1500000°	29' = 0.4833333°	49' = 0.81666666°
10' = 0.1666666°	30' = 0.5000000°	50' = 0.83333333°
11' = 0.1833333°	31' = 0.5166666°	51' = 0.85000000°
12' = 0.2000000°	32' = 0.5333333°	52' = 0.86666666°
13' = 0.2166666°	33' = 0.5500000°	53' = 0.88333333°
14' = 0.2333333°	34' = 0.5666666°	54' = 0.90000000°
15' = 0.2500000°	35' = 0.5833333°	55' = 0.91666666°
16' = 0.2666666°	36' = 0.6000000°	56' = 0.93333333°
17' = 0.2833333°	37' = 0.6166666°	57' = 0.95000000°
18' = 0.3000000°	38' = 0.6333333°	58' = 0.96666666°
19' = 0.3166666°	39' = 0.6500000°	59' = 0.98333333°
20' = 0.3333333°	40' = 0.6666666°	60' = 1.00000000°

Second and Degree		
10" = 0.00277777°	20" = 0.0055555°	30" = 0.00833333°
40" = 0.01111111°	50" = 0.0138888°	60" = 0.01666666°

This tell us that each year of life, for a house of size 24°23′, takes up 4°03′50′ of zodiacal arc. Adding this to the 3rd house cusp we can get the year point locations:

Age 12 = 25 VIR 37 (the 3rd house cusp)
Age 13 = Age 12 + 4°03′50″ = 25 VIR 37 + 4°04′ = 29 VIR 41
Age 14 = Age 13 + 4°03′50″ = 29 VIR 41 + 4°04′ = 3 LIB 45
Age 15 = Age 14 + 4°03′50″ = 3 LIB 45 + 4°04′ = 7 LIB 49
Age 16 = Age 15 + 4°03′50″ = 7 LIB 49 + 4°04′ = 11 LIB 53
Age 17 = Age 16 + 4°03′50″ = 11 LIB 53 + 4°04′ = 15 LIB 57
Age 18 = Age 17 + 4°03′ 50″ = 15 LIB 57 + 4°03′ = 20 LIB 00

20 LIB 00 is also the cusp of the next house, the 4th house.

The last year point calculation used 4° 03′ instead of 4° 04′ because the actual degree interval of 4° 03′ 50″ was rounded up to 4° 04′. The last line of the calculations above was lowered one minute to compensate for that rounding.

Taking another house as an example, let us do the same set of calculations on the 4th house:

The 4th house size is 50°05′; 1/6 of 50°05′ is 8°20′50″.

Therefore, the age arc for the 4th house, which has a size of 50°05′, is 8°20′50″. The individual year points can be calculated as before:

Age 18 occurs at the cusp of the 4th house which is at 20 LIB 00
Age 19 = Age 18 + 8°20′50″ = 20 LIB 00 + 8°20′50″ = 28 LIB 21
Age 20 = Age 19 + 8°20′50″ = 28 LIB 21 + 8°20′50″ = 6 SCO 42
Age 21 = Age 20 + 8°20′50″ = 6 SCO 42 + 8°20′50″ = 15 SCO 3
Age 22 = Age 21 + 8°20′50″ = 15 SCO 3 + 8°20′50″ = 24 SCO 24
Age 23 = Age 22 + 8°20′50″ = 24 SCO 24 + 8°20′50″ = 2 SAG 45
Age 24 = Age 23 + 8°20′50″ = 2 SAG 45 + 8°20′50″ = 10 SAG 5

Age 24 also occurs at the cusp of the next house, the 5th house.

Similar types of computations will produce the year point arcs for the other ages in life. Using these year point arcs is a useful way of determining where in the horoscope your AP is for the year. This type of computation should be performed for each year and once these calculations are done you will have a list of the zodiacal positions where your AP is for all your birthdays.

● Calculation of an Aspect to a Planetary Position

In our example, Venus is in the 9th house at 4 ARI 41. The cusp of the 9th house is 25 PSC 37 and the cusp of the 10th house (the MC) is 20 ARI 00. Since the 9th house will be the same size as the 3rd house, and the years will be symmetrical about the house points, we can copy our information from the 3rd house that was calculated on page 221 and modify it for the 9th house by inserting the opposite signs of the zodiac:

Age 48 = 25 PSC 37
Age 49 = Age 12 + 4°03′50″ = 25 PSC 37 + 4°04′ = 29 PSC 41
Age 50 = Age 13 + 4°03′50″ = 29 PSC 41 + 4°04′ = 3 ARI 45
Age 51 = Age 14 + 4°03′50″ = 3 ARI 45 + 4°04′ = 7 ARI 49
Age 52 = Age 15 + 4°03′50″ = 7 ARI 49 + 4°04′ = 11 ARI 53
Age 53 = Age 16 + 4°03′50″ = 11 ARI 53 + 4°04′ = 15 ARI 57
Age 54 = Age 17 + 4°03′50″ = 15 ARI 57 + 4°03′ = 20 ARI 00

20 ARI 00 is also the cusp of the next house, the 10th house.

Since Venus is at 4 ARI 41, the conjunction of the AP with Venus will be reached between the 50th and 51st years of life. The number of degrees in this year has already been determined to be 4°03′50″ (see page 000). It will take 365.25 days for the AP to travel this number of degrees. **The number of degrees that the AP travels in one day** can be determined from the following calculation:

4°03′50″ = 4.06388888° (determined before)
4.06388888° ÷ 365.25 days = 0.0111263° per day, or 0°00′40″ per day (using the same type of calculation logic as shown on page 19)

Thus, the AP moves at about the rate of 40″ of zodiacal arc per day while travelling through either the 3rd or the 9th houses. Now we must determine the distance from the nearest point to Venus, and then divide that arc distance by the movement of 40″ of arc per day to get the number of days it will take for the AP to travel from that year point date to Venus. The procedure is:

$$
\begin{array}{rcl}
\text{Venus} & = & 4\ \text{ARI}\ 41 \\
\text{(subtracting) Age 50} & = & -\ 3\ \text{ARI}\ 45 \\
\hline
\text{The arc difference} & = & 0°\qquad 56'
\end{array}
$$

This tells us that these is 0°56' of zodiacal arc between the point where the AP will be on the 50th birthday and where Venus is natally located. Since we have already determined that the AP is traveling at the rate of 40″ per day, we can convert the 56' to seconds by multiplying it by 60. Doing this we get:

$$56 \text{ minutes of arc} = 3360 \text{ seconds of arc}$$

Dividing 3360 seconds of arc by 40″ of arc movement of the AP/day, we get:

$$3360 \div 40 = 84 \text{ days}$$

Adding 84 days to the birthday, which is May 10th, we will find the date when the AP is conjunct natal Venus. We know that May has 31 days, and therefore there are 21 days left in May after the birthday. June has 30 days, and July has 31 days in the month. The total of 21 + 30 + 31 is 82 days. We have to stretch to 84 days, which is two more beyond July 31, so the date that the AP would reach Venus is August 2, in the 50th year of life.

● Calculation of the AP on a Particular Date

Suppose we wish to know where the AP was (*i.e.*, the sign and house position) for September 14th, 1960. Going back to the calculations that we have done previously (see pages 218 and 221), we first determine that this date, September 14th, 1960 occurs in the 18th year of life. Therefore the AP will have just passed the 4th house cusp (the IC) on the previous birthday, May 10th, 1960. We can see that the AP will have just passed the IC which is at 20 LIB 00. We must count the number of days from the birthdate to September 14th. Doing this we find the date of September 14th, 1960 is exactly 21 days (for the rest of May) + 30 days (for the month of June) + 31 days (for the month of July) + 31 days (for the month of August) + 14 days for the September portion away. Adding these days we get:

$$21 + 30 + 31 + 31 + 14 = 127 \text{ days}$$

That is, September 14th is 127 days away from May 10th.

Since the AP moves through the 4th house at the rate of speed of 8°20′50″ (see page 221 for this calculation) we can get the number of degrees per day that the AP is traveling through the 4th (or 10th) house. Doing this calculation we get the following result:

$$8°20′50″ = 8.3472222°$$

Dividing 8.3472222° by 365.25 we can get the number of degrees a day that the AP is moving through the house, which is:

$$8.3472222° \div 365.25 = 0.0228534° \text{ per day}$$
or 0°01′22.27″ per day of travel by the AP through the 4th house

Multiplying this daily rate of travel by the number of days between the birthdate and the target date we get:

$$0.0228534° \times 127 \text{ days} = 2.9023818°,$$
or 2°54′8.5″ motion in 127 days

This is the arc distance that the AP has moved in 127 days in a house of this size. Adding this distance (rounded) of 2°54′ to the AP location on the 18th birthday we get: 20 LIB 00 + 2°54′ = 22 LIB 54. Therefore, the AP is at 22 LIB 54 on September 14th, 1960.

● Determining When the Zodiacal Sign Changes Occur

Suppose we wish to know on what date the AP changes from the sign of LIBRA to the sign of SCORPIO. We can follow a set of calculations very similar to the ones used for determining when the AP would reach the planet Venus. In this example we realize that the AP must travel from the 4th house cusp, which is at 20 LIB 00 to 00 SCO 00. This is a distance of 10 degrees, exactly. In the 4th house we have already determined that the AP is traveling at a rate of 8°20'50" per year, or 0.0228534° per day (see previous example). Since the sign of Scorpio will be reached between the 19th and the 20th year, we know that we have to measure between 28 LIB 21 and 6 SCO 42 in the 19th year of life. See page 221 for these numbers which have been previously explained. The distance, in zodiacal degrees between 28 LIB 21 and 00 SCO 00, is found by subtracting the two values: 00 SCO 00 - 28 LIB 21 = 1°39' of arc difference.

Converting this (as before in the Venus example) to seconds of arc, we get: 1°39' = 5940 seconds of arc. Dividing the number of seconds of arc by the daily arc travel in the 4th house, which is 1'22.27" (or 82.27" of arc travel per day for the AP through the 4th house) we get:

$$5940 \text{ seconds of arc} \div 82.27" \text{ of arc/day} =$$
$$\text{(about) 72 days of time}$$

Therefore the sign of SCORPIO will be reached about 72 days after the 19th birthday. Calculating the days (as in the example before) we get 21 days for the rest of May, and 30 days for June. This has used 51 days. If we add the 31 days for July we will have used 82 days, which is more than we are looking to use, so the date the AP reaches 00 SCO 00 must be in the month of July in the 19th year. Since May has contributed 21 days to us, and June has given 30 days, then we have 72 - (30 + 21) = 72 - 51 = 21 days yet to account for. Therefore, on or about the date of July 21, in the 19th year of life, 1961 in this example, the AP will cross from LIBRA into the zodiacal sign of SCORPIO.

● Conclusion

At first glance the calculations seem a bit more formidable than they really are in practice. The calculation of when the AP reaches and activates the different parts of the chart is not very difficult or time consuming. With a little bit of practice you can easily master the techniques for doing these calculations. The following layouts and reviews of these steps may be of further help to you. Use them for your own practice.

House Size Calculation

1. Cusp of the 2nd House - Cusp of the 1st House = 1st House Size
   1st House Size = _____ - _____ = _____

2. Cusp of the 3rd House - Cusp of the 2nd House = 2nd House Size
   2nd House Size = _____ - _____ = _____

3. Cusp of the 4th House - Cusp of the 3rd House = 3rd House Size
   3rd House Size = _____ - _____ = _____

4. Cusp of the 5th House - Cusp of the 4th House = 4th House Size
   4th House Size = _____ - _____ = _____

5. Cusp of the 6th House - Cusp of the 5th House = 5th House Size
   5th House Size = _____ - _____ = _____

6. Cusp of the 7th House - Cusp of the 6th House = 6th House Size
   6th House Size = _____ - _____ = _____

7. Cusp of the 8th House - Cusp of the 7th House = 7th House Size
   7th House Size = _____ - _____ = _____

8. Cusp of the 9th House - Cusp of the 8th House = 8th House Size
   8th House Size = _____ - _____ = _____

9. Cusp of the 10th House - Cusp of the 9th House = 9th House Size
   9th House Size = _____ - _____ = _____

10. Cusp of the 11th House - Cusp of the 10th House = 10th House
    Size
    10th House Size = _____ - _____ = _____

11. Cusp of the 12th House - Cusp of the 11th House = 11th House
    Size
    11th House Size = _____ - _____ = _____

12. Cusp of the 1st House - Cusp of the 12th House = 12th House Size
    12th House Size = _____ - _____ = _____

Year Point Calculations

1. Determine the House Size in degrees and minutes   _____

2. Convert this number to whole degrees   _____

3. Divide this house size by 6   _____

4. Convert this answer to degrees, minutes and seconds   _____

5. Add the result (line 4) to the cusp to get the six different year points, as shown in the examples before:

Year Point #1 = House Cusp + the number from line 4 above

_____ + _____ = _____

Year Point #2 = Year Point #1 + the number from line 4 above

_____ + _____ = _____

Year Point #3 = Year Point #2 + the number from line 4 above

_____ + _____ = _____

Year Point #4 = Year Point #3 + the number from line 4 above

_____ + _____ = _____

Year Point #5 = Year Point #4 + the number from line 4 above

_____ + _____ = _____

Year Point #6 = Year Point #5 + the number from line 4 above

_____ + _____ = _____

Aspects to Planets, Points, IP, Sign Cusps

1. When you wish to know when an aspect will be exact, determine the arc distance from the nearest Year Point to the point or planet that you wish. Always measure ahead in the zodiac. Let us use a planet in the text here, but remember that the IP, a sign cusp, etc., will substitute equally well in this example.

Planet Position   =   _____

Year Point next previous   =   - _____

Distance to move   =   _____

2. Determine the speed that the AP is moving through the house: House Cusp at far end of house - House cusp at near end of House = Number of degrees in the House:

_____ - _____ = _____ (degrees in House)

3. Number of degrees of daily travel for the AP is the answer from No. 2, above. Divide this by 365.25:

_____ ÷ 365.25 = _____ (degrees AP moves/day)

4. Distance to move (from step 1), divided by AP speed in degrees (from step 3, above) gives the number of days from the birthdate to the target date:

_____ ÷ _____ = _____ (days from birthdate)

5. Add this number of days to the birthdate to get the target date.

Determine For Any Date Where The AP Is

1. When you wish to know where the AP is on any particular day, determine the number of days from the last birthday to this target date.

_____ + _____ = _____ (days from birthdate)

2. Take this number of days from #1 above, and multiply it by the speed that the AP is moving through the house the AP is in:

_____ × _____ = _____ (arc to move from birthdate)

3. Find the AP year point position on the birthdate: _____

4. Add 2 and 3 answers (from above) together:

_____ + _____ = _____ (AP position on target date)

Days in Life When the Cusps, IPs and LPs are Exact

		Days after Birth			Days after Birth
1st House Cusp	=	0	7th House Cusp	=	13149
IP	=	837.5	IP	=	13986.5
LP	=	1354	LP	=	14503
2nd House Cusp	=	191.5	8th House Cusp	=	15340.5
IP	=	3029	IP	=	16178
LP	=	3545.5	LP	=	16694.5
3rd House Cusp	=	4383	9th House Cusp	=	17532
IP	=	5220.5	IP	=	18365.5
LP	=	5737	LP	=	18886
4th House Cusp	=	6574.5	10th House Cusp	=	19723.5
IP	=	7412	IP	=	20561
LP	=	7928.5	LP	=	20177.5
5th House Cusp	=	8766	11th House Cusp	=	21915
IP	=	9603.5	IP	=	22752.5
LP	=	10120	LP	=	23269
6th House Cusp	=	10957.5	12th House Cusp	=	24106.5
IP	=	11795	IP	=	24944
LP	=	12311.5	LP	=	25460.5

Worksheet for Your Natal Chart

Zodiacal Location		Zodiacal Location	
1st House Cusp	= _____	7th House Cusp	= _____
IP	= _____	IP	= _____
LP	= _____	LP	= _____
2nd House Cusp	= _____	8th House Cusp	= _____
IP	= _____	IP	= _____
LP	= _____	LP	= _____
3rd House Cusp	= _____	9th House Cusp	= _____
IP	= _____	IP	= _____
LP	= _____	LP	= _____
4th House Cusp	= _____	10th House Cusp	= _____
IP	= _____	IP	= _____
LP	= _____	LP	= _____
5th House Cusp	= _____	11th House Cusp	= _____
IP	= _____	IP	= _____
LP	= _____	LP	= _____
6th House Cusp	= _____	12th House Cusp	= _____
IP	= _____	IP	= _____
LP	= _____	LP	= _____

Bibliography

Bailey, A. *Esoteric Astrology.* NY: Lucis Trust, 1979.

Brunton, Paul. *The Quest of the Overself.* York Beach, ME: Samuel Weiser, 1970; and London: Rider, 1970.

Ellenberger, H.F. *The Discovery of the Unconscious.* NY: Basic Books, 1970.

Erikson, Erik. *Childhood and Society.* NY: Norton, 1964.

———. *Identity and the Life Cycles.* NY: Norton, 1980.

Freud, S. and C.G. Jung. *The Freud/Jung Letters.* Edited by William McGuire, translated by Ralph Manheim and R.F.C. Hull. Bollingen Series, XCIV. Princeton, NJ: Princeton University Press, 1976.

Huber, Bruno and Louise. *The Astrological Houses: A Psychological View of Man and His World.* York Beach, ME: Samuel Weiser, 1984.

Huber, Louise. *Reflections and Meditations on the Signs of the Zodiac.* Tempe, AZ: American Federation of Astrologers, 1984.

Jones, Ernest. *The Life and Work of Sigmund Freud.* NY: Basic Books, 1961.

Jung, C.G. *Selected Letters of C.G. Jung, 1909-1961.* Selected and edited by Gerhard Adler, in collaboration with Aniela Jaffe. Princeton, NJ: Princeton University Press, 1984.

———. *Memories, Dreams, Reflections.* Edited by Aniela Jaffe. NY: Random House, 1965.

———. *Word and Image.* Edited by Aniela Jaffe. Bollingen Series, XCVII:2. Princeton, NJ: Princeton University Press, 1970.

Krishnamurti, J. *Freedom from the Known*. Krishnamurti Foundation, 1973.

Levinson, Daniel J. *The Seasons of a Man's Life*. NY: Alfred A. Knopf, 1978.

Ruperti, Alexander. *Cycles of Becoming*. Reno, NV: CRCS Publications, 1978.

Russell, Bertrand. *The Autobiography of Bertrand Russell*. London: Allen & Unwin, 1978.